Is It Genuine?

W. CRAWLEY

IS IT GENUINE?

*A Guide to the Identification
of Eighteenth-Century English Furniture*

HART PUBLISHING COMPANY, INC. · NEW YORK CITY

To the anonymous person who offered me a substantial sum not to print this book.

Contents

List of Illustrations

The photographs in Part IV Birth of an Antique *were taken by Roger Wood with the exception of Plates I and II which are by A. J. Rowell.*

The photographs in the chapter entitled "The Museum of Naughty Pieces"—*Illustrations 86 through 103—for obvious reasons carry no ascription.*

Is It Genuine?

Preface

There is a growing interest in old things, whether furniture, china or silver. This book has been written to help those whose interest is in eighteenth-century English furniture and to enable them to check that what they have, or are considering buying, is what it purports to be.

There is one way of vetting antique furniture: you can check the piece for the detail and characteristics of style, maker, material, date, etc. that will show that the piece could be what it is supposed to be. Here you are pitting your wits against the expert fakers of the last 150 years. Only the expert will start from scratch using old wood from broken period pieces or pieces too large to get into modern homes. The commonest deception of all is the 'made' antique, when a piece is taken to pieces and reassembled as something else. How this can be done is illustrated in Part Four: Birth of an antique. But spotting the expertly made-up fake calls for profound knowledge that only years of study and experience of handling furniture can give.

There are, though, a number of principles and rules of their craft from which the cabinet-makers of the eighteenth century never departed and if you familiarise yourself with these, you will find that it is comparatively easy to tell when a piece is wrong.

This book illustrates and explains these principles and rules. The introduction discusses briefly the question of how much eighteenth-century furniture there is and Part One describes how the book came to be written. Part Two illustrates what can be done to alter furniture. Part Three describes, in alphabetical order, the characteristic details of eighteenth-century furniture and special things to look out for when examining pieces. In Part Five the pieces themselves are described, again in alphabetical order. Equipped with this knowledge, the answer to the question 'Is It Genuine?' will be more easily and authoritatively answered.

I should like to thank all of those who have provided photographs which are acknowledged individually in the list of illustrations.

The pieces illustrated are of course all genuine except where expressly and categorically stated to the contrary. Perhaps it should be added that in laying down criteria for judging the genuineness of pieces, it has been necessary to be somewhat dogmatic and the possibility is recognized that some pieces which do not fulfil all the criteria might nevertheless be genuine. But they should be regarded as exceptional.

INTRODUCTION

How much Eighteenth-Century English Furniture is there?

The population of England at the end of the eighteenth century, the great age of English furniture, has been estimated as less than $12\frac{1}{2}$ million, made up of about two million families. Of these, less than 140,000 families were in a position to pay the prices charged by Chippendale and other craftsmen for their furniture. How many of these 140,000 can have required to furnish or refurnish during the century? Some people consider that no more than 2,000 families, if as many, could have afforded the London-made furniture of their day, for, of course, all the artist craftsmen in this trade soon made their way to London. There must be now nearly 2,000 houses in the United States of America alone whose owners consider that they have one or more rooms furnished with eighteenth-century English furniture. And then there are all the museums in Britain, the United States, the Commonwealth and on the Continent of Europe, to say nothing of the antique shops of many countries all with displays of eighteenth-century furniture. Apart from these there is a multitude of private collectors all with pieces they are convinced are Chippendale, Sheraton, Hepplewhite or at any rate eighteenth-century furniture. Where did it all come from?

Part of the answer, of course, lies in the fact that, at the same time as they were making their monstrosities, the Victorians were also busy making reproduction Chippendale and Sheraton for instance (at any rate up to 1897), and now these pieces are often put forward as the genuine article, in many cases by those who do not know the difference. In 1909, the Bureau of Manufactures, Department of Commerce and Labor in the U.S.A., published a pamphlet dealing largely with the manufacture of reproduction furniture in England and Scotland. The author of *The Lure of the Antique* (1910), Walter A. Dyer, recommends American collectors to study this pamphlet carefully before making a purchase. The rest of the answer is supplied by such stories as that of a man I knew, who, from 1937 until 1948 (with six years in the services in between), made over three hundred Chippendale chairs and nearly two hundred Chippendale wing-chairs which were sent to sales and salerooms all over the country. These chairs, all of them sold as 'genuine', fetched enough in this short space of time for him to retire. His last set of six single chairs and two armchairs cost him £120 to make and fetched £3,800, and his last wing-chair, which was covered in gros point, cost £65 (including needlework) and fetched £1,200.

A favourite practice is to manufacture sofa-tables to eighteenth-century design, as well as Regency and Hepplewhite chairs, dining tables, mirrors, brass beds and carriage-lamps. Both here and abroad Victorian and Edwardian pieces are changed into Chippendale and Sheraton by altering mouldings, adding cockbeading to front edges of drawers, and either re-veneering or removing inlays. Some London West End shops now send pieces to Italy, where labour is cheap, for this type of face-lift. It pays, when there is not enough to fill a van, for them to send smaller consignments by air (there and back), which shows that the profit margin must be considerable indeed.

The truth is that there are very few genuine pieces of eighteenth-century furniture of any importance available for sale and, almost without exception, they are known to the few experts in the same way as rare precious stones are known to the merchants of Hatton Garden. This does not apply to bedroom furniture, but rather to the finer pieces made for drawing-room, library and boudoir.

There is probably not enough genuine eighteenth-century antique furniture for sale to keep more than one shop going in London, and another in the North of England. Before the war there was not enough eighteenth-century furniture available for even *one* antique fair more than every other year. Now they can be held regularly up and down the country, partly because as time goes on more furniture qualifies to be called an antique.

Is It Genuine?

PART ONE

*How this book came
to be written*

When I left school in 1934 my father apprenticed me to a firm of cabinet-makers. For seven years I was to learn the craft of those who had worked for Chippendale, Sheraton and Adam, and I was excited at the prospect. The firm was mainly engaged in restoring damaged antiques, mostly eighteenth-century pieces, and in making copies of others, and soon I had fallen in love with eighteenth-century English furniture. I admired and envied the talent and craftsmanship that had gone into it, and before long I was telling myself that I was going to do work as good. To reach this standard I had to know my craft as well as the cabinet-makers had theirs; so I read everything about it I could find. I studied the design books of those who to me were 'the masters', and I went to museums and big houses open to the public in order to study their pieces and examined the damaged pieces my firm repaired so as to see exactly how they were made.

Gradually, I became quite an efficient cabinet-maker and began to specialize in bachelor chests. But I was still learning and improving. When you are actually making similar pieces with your own hands you obtain a wonderful insight not only into the technique and the why and wherefore of it, but also into the possibilities – and limitations – of your materials.

In those days we apprentices, like all young people learning a craft, trade or business, were not considered worth much of a wage until we could really do what was wanted of us, which we were usually able to do long before the fact was recognized in cash; as a result, we were chronically hard up. In our spare time we made little pieces such as jewel caskets. The early ones we gave to our families, the later and better pieces we used to sell. As we became better craftsmen we became more ambitious and bought old bits of unwanted furniture for the timber and made these up into something different. That done, we would get a hawker's licence, rent a one-day pitch at East Street Market, Walworth or Petticoat Lane and try to sell our piece. I was fortunate: in return for washing my boss's car, I was given the run of his workshop in my spare time so that I had all the lathes, tools and aids I could wish.

One of my comparatively early efforts in furniture-making was a kidney-shaped satinwood dressing-table, which I duly took to East Street Market. In my eyes my table was a piece well worthy of Sheraton and a good deal more valuable than the £6 I was asking for it. It had taken me most of my spare time for the previous four months to make it and a lot of love, skill and enthusiasm had gone into it.

Luck was with me and I sold it and never thought to see it again. A few years ago, however, when going round an antiques fair, I saw it on a stand there. I knew the firm well and congratulated them on having such a nice piece. I was told that it was their main exhibit for the show and that they were asking £700 for it. It was pleasant to have my own secret estimate of its excellence thus confirmed. And to know that during the fair they sold it!

In the days of my apprenticeship eighteenth-century furniture did not often turn up at sales and there was only one antique fair in London every two years. As a result, the fact that a dealer, who had bought at auction or privately three ordinary chairs and one armchair of the period, should come to us and order a matching armchair and three ordinary ones, and that subsequently he would be fortunate enough to have a complete set of six chairs and two armchairs for sale in his shop, scarcely linked up in our minds and certainly did not worry our youthful consciences. When you are earning fifty shillings a week, the business of making ends meet, and getting something out of life at the same time, leaves you little time for worrying about ethical niceties of that kind. Anyway, my firm never pretended that a piece was what it was not. We just accepted commissions to repair, restore or copy. What the person who paid for the job did subsequently was not our concern and we did not feel responsible. Should our copies be good enough to deceive the expert that was a feather in our craftsman's cap, if we ever thought of it at all, but we ourselves never submitted them to the test. We got a fair price for our work, made no outrageous profit and deceived no one.

My call-up papers came a few months before my apprenticeship was technically at an end, but I had then achieved a high enough standard to be considered a master and the last few months were remitted. The next four years I spent in India and Burma where I happened to come across several fellow cabinet-makers of roughly my own age, and it was while talking shop that we first began to concern ourselves with the ethics of the trade. We argued at length, as the young will, and decided that, after the war, we would set up on our own and never ourselves put reproductions into sales as antiques.

On being demobbed I found that it was going to be anything but easy to fulfil this ambition. New furniture could only be bought on dockets and 'timber' furniture (for breaking up) was very difficult to obtain. So, too, were cabinet-maker's tools and lathes, while there were so many restrictions on where you could instal machinery and so little workshop accommodation available that I almost despaired. Contacting my army cabinet-maker friends, I found that they were all in the same state. One had even taken a baker's round.

In the end I had to go back to my old job and restore, repair and convert according to instructions given to my employer by antique dealers. I began to give classes on antique furniture, hoping that by imparting some of my knowledge, I would help to protect the amateur and prevent him being taken in by the 'naughty' piece. 'Naughty' is the term used in the trade for a piece that has been converted, married (see p. 27) or tampered with, without the alterations being declared. Unfortunately, teaching is a double-edged weapon, for although members of the public are taught the elements of craftsmanship that enable them to detect fakes, instruction can also open the eyes of any junkshop owner so inclined to what can be done.

In 1939, I happened to have a fair amount

of satinwood, most of it from a Victorian wardrobe, and I decided to do something with it. Working in my spare time for several months I made a very nice semi-circular commode, a copy of a popular eighteenth-century design. It had its faults, of course: for instance I had no lock for the door and had taken that (obviously Victorian) off the bottom door of the wardrobe. This was too heavy and wide, but it had to do. I fixed it on the stile of the door, where it was in the vertical instead of the horizontal and so big it overlapped the stile. But never mind, this fault could not be seen from the outside and with the door shut the piece looked perfect. Well-pleased, or at least quite pleased, with myself and my handiwork, I got my hawker's licence, loaded the commode onto a handcart on the Sunday morning and took it through the streets to East Street, Walworth. All morning I stood beside my treasure, but unlike my first piece, nobody would buy it.

I had to take it home.

The next Sunday I trundled it all the way to Petticoat Lane, through pouring rain. I found my pitch, set up my beautiful commode which I priced at £10. The rain continued to fall. I was offered £8·75 and, wet and nearly despondent, I did not dare refuse.

The next time I saw my commode was in 1949 in a shop which is no longer there. After that I used to see it here and there in the West End shops, as one dealer sold it to another, while the price asked for it escalated. I wonder where it is now?

One of my classes is about veneers and inlays. Some years ago, to illustrate that walnut veneer is always found on an oak (or pine) body and that you cannot satisfactorily fake herring-bone inlay, I bought a tallboy with walnut veneer and an oak grandfather clock and bureau-bookcase. The class and I stripped the veneer off the tallboy and put it on the clock and the bureau-bookcase, providing the latter with herring-bone inlay. I then pointed out that anyone with a knowledge of the craft would see that the inlay had been relaid. To demonstrate this I took the bureau-bookcase and the clock to the home of a friend and asked her to try and dispose of them using the techniques of those people (mostly individuals, not firms) who make reproduction eighteenth-century furniture as like the original as they can (i.e. fakes), in the hope of selling them for the large prices the rare genuine article always fetches. The procedure is to ring up a firm of auctioneers, describe the piece that 'has been in the family some time' and which 'we' are now thinking of selling. In all probability you will be invited to send the piece in and then perhaps an excited saleroom 'expert' will write or even telephone, pronouncing the piece Sheraton, Chippendale, Queen Anne or whatever and offering to put it in a forthcoming sale. Naturally, you accept. In the catalogue it will be described as Chippendale, or whatever the expert thought it was, the saleroom of course being protected by its condition of sale which disclaims all responsibility etc. And that will be that. This is what my friend did. She put the two pieces in her living-room, got in touch with a firm of auctioneers to which she described the pieces but without attributing them to any period or style, and was duly invited to send them in, which she did. But instead of being told that the pieces were comparatively valueless, as the inlay was relaid and the veneer of recent application, she received an enthusiastic letter offering to sell the pieces for her. They were duly included in a sale, catalogued as Queen Anne, and fetched £850 and over £300 respectively.

When a person – for instance a widow moving into a smaller place – wants to sell a piece or pieces that she or her husband had bought, the first step is often to ring up the person from whom the pieces were obtained and offer them there. All too frequently the firm concerned will be 'overstocked' with that particular kind of piece and will not wish to buy – at any price. The seller then rings up another firm. They send a man round, he sees that the piece is a fake or a conversion but, as he has many such on his own conscience, he cannot afford to give the other fellow away, so he either gives excuses for not even making an offer or makes one so low that he knows it will be refused. In this way, it is possible for a puzzled seller to call in twenty or thirty persons, as did one lady.

Two of the firms she approached, asked me – in my capacity as independent outside consultant, which I still am – to see the pieces, of which there were several. She had all the receipts and these totalled £11,000; yet, apart from one armchair, nothing she had was genuine. None of the others who came to see the furniture (and refused to buy it) had been prepared to tell her the truth, but she learned it from me; it was highly unpalatable and difficult to stomach and she took some convincing, but in the end, she realized that I was right and handed the matter over to her solicitor. The two firms who had sold her husband the pieces settled out of court.

My real 'conversion' came in 1952, when one day in a shop in Chelsea I saw thirty-seven pieces of so-called eighteenth-century furniture that over the years I had helped to alter and convert and they were all being offered as genuine original pieces. I had been shaken by the ease with which the grandfather clock and bureau-bookcase had gone through the sale rooms and into an antique fair, but this sight convinced me that I must stop all cabinet-maker's work, which

I could see was tantamount to aiding and abetting, and since then I have not made or restored a piece.

I had intended to make a clean break, but once you have been in any way concerned with a 'racket' it is only possible to achieve that, as I now see, if you transfer your endeavours to a completely different occupation in a different part of the country. As I am one of the few who really know 'how to do it', people have now and again asked for advice and guidance. When a friend of many years standing comes and tells you he has been landed with a so-called period piece that is not convincing and asks you to help and tell him what he should do to make it look right, what can you say? And when he offers you a small commission on what he eventually gets for it, and you think of the rent and the rates and the rising cost of living, it is extraordinarily difficult to say 'no'; so being human, often I have told them what to do and how; however, I have not with my own hands made, or helped to make a 'naughty' piece, but have confined myself to consultant work, inspecting pieces and valuing for private persons, firms and insurance companies.

Naturally I still see 'my' pieces here and there. They turn up in the salerooms, West End shops, or at antique fairs. Not long ago I watched a Queen Anne kneehole-desk being sold for £850. It was one that in 1951 I had helped to convert from a Queen Anne chest-of-drawers. The chest cost the antique dealer £55 and the bill for the alteration was £38. At about the same time, I converted a wardrobe into a breakfront-bookcase. For this we had to buy old prints to get the right old glass to make the panes in the doors. The customer for whom the job was done put the piece into a sale, where it was bought by an antique dealer for £3,500. It was a well-made piece and worth £300 or £400, but not £3,500.

You can almost say that in the antique trade today a little knowledge is a dangerous thing and that it pays much better to know nothing, and so be able, with hand on heart, to assure your customer that to the best of your 'expert' knowledge the piece is genuine this, that or the other, as the man who sold it to you said it was, or as it was described (without responsibility) in the auctioneer's catalogue.

Are all these 'naughty' pieces fakes? Yes and no. A fake is a piece of furniture especially made to be mistaken for what it is not. Up to the last war, in order to deceive the experts, a fake had to be made with considerable craftsmanship and knowledge of the subject, and, like the paintings of Van Megeeren, many of them were almost works of art in themselves. The cabinet-maker will easily detect errors in craftsmanship, but there is more to it than that and it requires not only a thorough knowledge of the craft of the eighteenth-century cabinet-maker, of his tools and technique, but also a knowledge of timber great enough to be able to say whether a piece of mahogany comes from the West Indies or Central America. You must know how logs were sawn in the eighteenth century, recognize the marks of the eighteenth-century tools, have a pair of callipers to measure the subtle difference in thickness inevitable in sawing and planing by hand, but not found when this is done mechanically (even the best faker falls for the temptation to save himself work by using machines) and most of the other 'tricks' of the trade by which alone the expert can pronounce for or against a piece. To acquire this knowledge calls for years of application and experience.

It is not my intention to try to instruct the reader in the technicalities that are involved here. It is a complex subject that would take a whole book to itself and as these expert fakes have mostly found permanent homes, the need for this knowledge will seldom, if ever, arise as far as the average collector is concerned. Remember, though, that there are a few things the faker, however, expert, cannot do: he cannot satisfactorily fake patination (see p. 64), nor can he get modern brass of the same colour (and composition) as eighteenth-century brass (see p. 56), so that such things as new handles, for instance made to the old design to complete the set, or to provide a whole new set, inevitably give themselves away. Nor can the faker reproduce the patches of discolouration in the timber around the heads of nails and screws that are the inevitable result of oxidization, caused by two hundred years of changes of humidity and temperature in rooms (see p. 67). Even if the faker has used old nails and screws, as he will if he knows his job, the discerning eye will be able to tell from the discolouration, or lack of it, what has happened (see p. 63).

These are about the amateur's only safeguards against the master faker. But very few fakers will have the necessary knowledge or will go to all this trouble today, when it is so easy to deceive people, and 'antique' furniture is being mass-produced. In fact, there is now a minor, less lucrative but still very paying form of fakery: for Victorian furniture, which in recent years has acquired antique status, is now being widely made.

The amateur should remember:
1. That no auctioneer will accept any responsibility that goods sold under his hammer are what they are described as being, so that it is entirely up to the intending purchaser to satisfy himself that the lot he wants is genuine and correctly described before he bids for it. If it is not, he alone is

responsible. Auctioneers only act as 'agents' of the seller.

2.　That when the contents of a house are auctioned on the premises, auctioneers often accept goods from other sources in order to fill up or make a whole day's sale. This is one of the great opportunities for those who today manufacture eighteenth-century furniture. Not only that, but dealers have been known to take a three-month lease of an empty house that is up for sale, furnish it with their 'antiques' (putting lots of books onto the piano, for instance, so that the castors make deep marks in the carpet and look as if they had been in that position for years, and then hold a sale of the 'contents of a private house'.

3.　That many an old family requiring money has had copies of its genuine eighteenth-century furniture made and then sold the originals, intending at some time to 'confess' and tell the family that the genuine pieces have gone; but often the seller has been too ashamed or has simply forgotten to do so before he died. The heirs, believing in good faith that they have inherited valuable furniture (for which there may even be receipts among the family papers), have then sent the reproduction stuff to be auctioned and, in the great majority of cases, have obtained wonderful prices for their pieces.

These reproductions, of course, are made by craftsmen and are themselves excellent pieces of furniture, furniture that anyone would be glad to live with provided he had not paid twenty or thirty times its value. (It only becomes 'fake', of course, if it is deliberately represented as being what it is not.)

When it comes to shops, the buyer should remember that those in charge are not always experts. In any particular field there are only a few experts. Some of these of course are in the trade but a good many are not and for example work for museums. The difficulty is to make sure that you have found a real expert before you accept any judgement.

One of the things that especially strikes the visitor to antique fairs is that almost everything looks brand new. It is all so glossy and perfectly polished, it might have been made yesterday. A piece's 'origins' may indeed be recent, but not as recent as that. This 'new' look is due to the fact that many, if not most big antique shops now re-polish the pieces they have for sale. First they strip the old polish and in doing so, of course, remove all patination: they then re-polish using the old method of wax polishing.

Those who do this maintain that they are doing no more than the person who cleans a picture; but is that so? Varnish and the dirt that accumulates on it are not essential parts of a picture, nor such important evidence of its age and origins, whereas the original polish on a piece of furniture was given in the workshop where it was made, and the patination (accumulated dirt and grease, see p. 64) is *essential* evidence of a piece's genuineness and age. People will tell you that the lack of it does not matter, provided everything else is right, but I cannot think otherwise than that to destroy such important evidence detracts considerably from the value of a piece.

Obviously any piece of furniture that is used runs the risk of being damaged and one cannot imagine a piece in daily use for over two hundred years coming through unscathed. Mostly it is the feet that suffer: brooms and now vacuum cleaners bump against them, and they bear the strain when a piece is dragged from one place to another instead of being lifted. And damage has to be made good. A home cannot house generations of children without there being accidents. Serious damage, such as is caused by a spilt corrosive, cigarette or cigar burn, may entail re-polishing and it may then look better to re-polish the whole; but even that is debatable, because re-polishing, say, a top demonstrates that it has been repaired, while leaving the patination elsewhere provides valuable evidence, though not necessarily proof, that the rest has not been tampered with.

Anyway, when a piece has been repaired it should be acknowledged and pointed out by the seller. Repairs are nearly always detectable, if not obvious, and it is up to the antique dealer to look for and draw attention to this detail which can vitally affect the value of a piece. If you stop to think: how many pieces of furniture *can* still be in their original or 'mint' condition as the trade calls it, after two hundred years of use? None. Even the best will have accumulated dirt on its back edges and where it has been handled, to give the patination that in advertisements I have seen described as 'original'! (The question of patination is most important and will crop up repeatedly through this book.)

Of course, these re-polished pieces, even if they have been repaired as well, are valuable and very well worth having. I would never discourage anyone from buying one for a sensible price; but it is very different with the innumerable other pieces that have been knocked together out of bits of old timber, the pieces that have been cut down in size, added-to, 'married' to another odd bit to make something quite different. Many of these have no value beyond that of the timber in them, not even an artistic one, for the need to preserve visible edges with patination on them imposes proportions that are often wrong. These are the pieces the trade calls 'naughty', not fakes or reproduction, just 'naughty', that is – tampered with.

Occasionally, no doubt, some eighteenth-century person would want a piece of furniture for a special purpose, or an eccentric would indulge a whim and have something made to his own design, but in the great majority of cases such pieces would be made locally and not ordered from Chippendale, Gillows or any other big London maker; so beware of the piece of which it is said none like it has ever been seen before, the 'hitherto unrecorded' and the 'very rare', when attributed to a great name. These pieces *can* be genuine, but the probability is that they are like the urn and globe stand which students of mine once made into a 'rare' washstand. Out of devilment, they put it into a London sale where a dealer bought it. Everyone was taken in and at the time of writing it stood in a north country gallery, with an indication that it was a Sheraton washstand of unusual type. A dealer *may* discover a unique piece that has been hidden away and forgotten for a hundred years, but it is most improbable and if you buy a piece he has never seen before, in all probability no one else will have either.

For many years I have been in a position to know of and to see in the making, thousands of 'naughty' pieces which today are bought and sold as antiques. I have a record of 53,714 pieces of furniture sold between March 1946 and February 1966, which are either altered or complete fakes. I know who bought the original pieces, who altered them and how, to whom they were sold, the dealers through whose hands they passed and what the purchaser finally paid for them. Even this record must be far from complete.

Fortunately, because of the limitations imposed by the materials themselves, most 'naughtiness' is relatively easy to spot. The faults are those of materials and craftsmanship, proportion and, of course, the absence of the inevitable signs of age: patination and rust around nail and screw heads.

I have written the book to help the reader

tell whether a piece of furniture he is told is eighteenth-century is so or not, to enable him to recognize pieces that have been altered, cut down in size, adapted or converted to another use. It will, I hope, help the private person who buys at auction or from antique shops. I hope, too, that it will bring home to the great number of people who have gone into the antique trade since the war the necessity of knowing what they buy and sell and help them to acquire this knowledge. It will also help people to adjust their insurance premiums – up or, in many cases, I am afraid, down.

My publishers thought that I ought to include a section on the periods and the makers, explaining their main characteristics and identification marks. The more I thought it over, however, the less inclined I was to consider this important. You will not be prevented from buying a fake or 'naughty' piece by knowing that Chippendale was the first to make the straight leg with five sides and that he put a C-scroll somewhere on all his carved pieces or that the characteristics of Adam furniture are the urn or ram's head (sometimes both) that appear on all his pieces – when all these are still being made in their hundreds.

It is no help to know that on all Queen Anne flat surfaces, the veneer is quartered, though it will be of immense value to know that if the herring-bone inlay around the quartering is level all round or countersunk, it must be wrong because after two hundred years this inlay must inevitably have lifted in places, owing to the effect of changes in temperature and humidity, and that the restorer cannot lay inlay in such a way as to imitate this.

The things that are right are explained in a great variety of books. But as the converter, the restorer and the faker know all this better than you and reproduce it all to the best of their ability, to know it leaves you no better able to detect the fake or 'naughty' piece. That you will only be able to do, if you know what is *wrong* and where to look for it, and that is what I am setting out to explain. When, after acquiring this basic knowledge, you go out to buy, remember that the real criteria are (a) how a piece was made, because eighteenth-century craftsmen did most things in only one way, the way they considered best for the job; and (b) what it was made with. If these are correct and all the important proportions of the piece are right and there is patination to prove age, then you won't go far wrong.

Many indications of a piece having been tampered with, for example, new sides to drawers, dovetails cut through, legs in two pieces, cannot be seen in a photograph and in many advertisements pieces look perfect, but when you realize what can be done to alter or give a piece a new appearance and how little of this is superficially evident, before buying a piece from a photograph only, you should ask yourself: how is it that a genuine eighteenth-century piece has not been snapped up the moment it came on the market? Why is it hanging fire to the extent that it is being advertised or offered to me? It may only be that the price asked is too steep for others to pay, but there might be another reason.

PART TWO

What can be done: Repairing, Restoring and Converting

As a man who has made a fortune by producing double-heighted corner cupboards once said, most antique dealers have little knowledge of the goods in which they deal and not much idea of what can be done to make pieces of furniture appear to be what they are not.

There is, in fact, little that a craftsman cannot do in the way of 'converting' one piece into another and one period into another: the tops of tallboys can be made into chests-of-drawers, the bottoms into dressing-tables, side tables, commodes and chests-of-drawers: chests-of-drawers can be made into kneehole-desks and dressing-tables; four-poster beds are made into tripod-tables, torchères, court cupboards and small buffets; cheval mirror stands are used for the end standards of sofa-tables; wardrobes are made into breakfront-bookcases and china-cabinets; centre tables into side tables; side tables into sideboards and commodes; settees into wing-, writing- and desk chairs; chairs into stools, etc. Victorian pedestal-desks, drum tables and chairs can be transformed into period pieces – the list is almost endless. But because the demand to-day is for small pieces to fit our smaller rooms and because eighteenth-century furniture on the whole was larger than is wanted today, the most common form of tampering has been, and is, to reduce a large to a small piece, both in length and depth. Where there are drawers, this calls for considerable skill.

The converter's argument is that he is improving a piece, when he takes one that is large or bulky and turns it into a smaller piece of a different kind more suited for the modern home. This might be true, if the piece was sold as, say 'a kneehole-desk made out of a Queen Anne chest-of-drawers' using only old timber, but the fact that the basis is a Queen Anne commode does not make the kneehole-desk Queen Anne. Nor does a kidney-shaped table made from a Victorian satinwood wardrobe in Sheraton style thereby become a Sheraton table. It is rather a question of labels: where these tell the truth and the price reflects the true value, this argument may be justified, provided the work put into the piece is of the requisite craftsmanship. But when after conversion, a piece is labelled what it is not, the situation is very different.

There is also the question of restoration. The man who restores anything – silver, porcelain, painting, furniture – is a craftsman and a lover of old things. He will, he must, take infinite pains with his work. The man who restores antique furniture has to know the whole technique of the craft and have a good all-round knowledge of all periods – early oak, walnut, mahogany and satinwood. He will be able to repair even bad damage and make the piece look perfectly sound without looking new. This is done by using old timbers from pieces for which no one has had a use, and which he buys to break up for their timber. Sometimes he will have to wait years for the right timber or veneer and if he gets it, no repolishing will be required. All he need do is to wax the piece and, if the repair has been expert, no one will be able to tell what has been done.

It is thus a question of the owner's integrity, whether or not he reveals what has been done. The piece remains valuable, but, of course, nothing like as valuable as if it had not had to be repaired.

On the other hand, most rescue operations are mere repairs, and not done so meticulously that they are not comparatively easy to detect.

Restoration or repair is, of course, very different to conversion, which today is the fate of most large pieces. Conversion often involves reduction in size and this means altering not only the height or width but also the depth, as this has to be roughly in proportion if the result is to look at all acceptable. How this is done is illustrated further on in the section *Birth of an Antique*.

In the case of a chest-of-drawers that has to be reduced in depth, the first thing is to remove all veneer from the carcase, usually by steaming. The back edge of the chest is then cut off and put aside, after which the requisite amount is cut off the top, sides and bottom; the back is then replaced. Next, the drawers have to be reduced in proportion. Here there are two methods: the better is that illustrated in *Birth of an Antique*, but where time and money are to be saved, the 'reducer'

will just cut through the scribe mark – that is the score in the wood on the sides made by the original cabinet-maker to show where the dovetails were to end; the required amount is then cut off the two sides and bottom, old gramophone needles dipped in wax are driven into the sides, and the front, with the original dovetails intact, is pressed on again (no glue is used, as this would leave a tell-tale mark). Of course, this is a flimsy join and a hard pull is likely to bring the front of such a drawer off in your hands. This operation means that the grain of the wood in the sides does not continue properly through the scribe mark, and the restorer will scratch grooves with a pin to simulate grain, which can be done very convincingly. If the piece has to be reduced in width as well as in depth, this involves removing the cock-beading from the drawers, and steaming the veneer off the fronts; the sides of the drawers are then cut off, leaving the dovetails intact. An equal amount is cut off either side of the front of the drawer, so that the lock is still left in the centre, the old handle holes are plugged, the veneers cut and glued back, the four edges of the front of the drawer are cock-beaded and a piece of plain veneer put on the inside face of the drawer to cover the holes which have been plugged; fresh holes are then drilled for the same, or other old handles, and none but an expert will know that anything has been done.

Chests-of-drawers can also be turned into kneehole-desks or dressing-tables by leaving the top drawer intact and cutting about a foot out of the centre of each of the three drawers underneath, making six very small drawers, each of which will have to have one new side. The back part of the space thus made is partially filled with a cupboard, leaving a recess for the knees, i.e. the kneehole that gives this kind of desk its name. The

1 The tallboy or double chest as designed by Hepplewhite.

2 How easy to make it into two of this

3 or even this.

new sides given to the drawers will not have any patination if they have been made from new timber or, even if made from old timber, not the same degree and pattern of patination as on the other (original) side.

Chests-of-drawers are also made out of the top or bottom part of a tallboy. The bottom part of a tallboy only requires the addition of a flat top, often obtained from the leaf of a dining table, to make it a chest-of-drawers, while the top part requires both a new top and a set of four feet. In the case of such conversions the show will often be given away by the number of drawers (the top part of a tallboy may have two small and three long drawers, but the bottom part nearly always has only three long drawers) and always by the lack of patination on the back edge of the top board, which will be an addition.

The chest-on-stand is a gift for the converter; the top part makes a chest-of-drawers and the bottom part a dressing-table or side table. The back stretcher rail of the bottom part will give the show away, however, because it will be straight – these rails were always made straight to provide the extra strength needed to support a heavy top part – whereas on a genuine dressing- or side table it would be curved.

In 1964 a restorer bought a chest-on-stand from a dealer for £65. He altered it as described above and put the result, a chest-of-drawers and a dressing-table, into an auction at which they were bought for just over £525 and just under £200 respectively – by the same dealer from whom the restorer had bought the original piece!

Bachelor chests with fold-over tops are in great demand. They are usually only 10″ deep. Now, some old Queen Anne chests-of-drawers are 2′ 6″ wide and 1′ 8″ deep (from front to back), so that the top of such an old chest divides nicely into two 10″ sections,

one of which will provide the flap that the 'genuine' bachelor chest must have. When the chest and its drawers have been reduced in depth, as described above, you have what appears to be the genuine thing.

Another method of obtaining a bachelor chest is to buy a walnut chest, reduce it to the right size, remove the top and replace it with the top of a walnut card-table. Or you can buy a walnut bureau, cut the writing section off completely just above the top drawer, reduce the drawers and carcase from front to back and use the flap of the bureau to provide the fold-over top.

Genuine bachelor chests of the early periods fetch £850 to £1,200, so they are well worth manufacturing.

Everybody wants chairs and there are probably more fakes among 'genuine period' chairs than among any other pieces. The basic 'raw material' is the settee, especially the chair-backed settee. The two-seat settee is simply cut in half and, if the restorer is not greedy, made into one chair; since it will have two original sides, the resulting fake will be almost undetectable. However, usually the converter is greedy and he will make two chairs, each of which will have a new side and two new legs.

Sometimes arms are added to a single chair to make it an armchair, despite the fact that the seat of an armchair is always wider than that of a single chair. (Usually by 2¼″–3″.)

Many Victorian chairs with ugly, turned legs are transformed into Sheraton chairs, for example, by having their round legs either replaced by square or tapered legs or sabre legs, or by being turned to a small diameter and boxed in with four pieces of mahogany in such a way that the inside tapers; this provides the appearance of a leg of the right period, but the bottom of the leg, where the tell-tale O of the original leg will still be visible inside the casing, has to be disguised. This is done with a piece of plain veneer or with a box castor (or both) – or with a dome of silence, a small metal disc with three lugs fixed in the bottom of the leg.

Bureaux and other large pieces can be reduced like chests-of-drawers. Very few, if any, period bureaux were made as small as 2′ 6″ wide, yet this is a size that today fetches the highest price. A 4′ 0″ William and Mary bureau can be bought for £140 to £160 and reduced to 2′ 6″ at a cost of £50 to £60, after which it will be worth £850 to £1200. Or, for £80, you could have a top part made transforming it into a bureau-bookcase which might fetch £950.

When a piece is reduced and the original handles retained, these will often give the show away by being out of proportion to the drawers to which they are fitted, since these are now smaller (see *Handles*). In these cases, too, the handles will either be too high up towards the top of the drawer or come too low down.

Breakfront-bookcases can be made out of secretaire-bookcases, bureau-bookcases or even chests-of-drawers to which wings and/ or a top are added. But most start life as a breakfront-wardrobe which is then reduced from front to back and has the panels of the top parts of the doors removed and replaced with glass, sometimes with old glass out of old framed prints. This operation was recently performed on a wardrobe bought for £38; the alterations and the fifty-two pieces of glass cost £103; the 'breakfront-bookcase' was then included among the contents of a private house which were to be auctioned, and at the sale it was bought by a dealer for nearly £2,000. A similar piece with doors to the waist and drawers below was bought in Devon for £8; the doors were glazed, the drawers removed and replaced with a pair of new doors making

a cupboard; the whole was reduced from front to back by 10″. The conversion made it into a 'china-cabinet' – as which it was sold at an antique fair for over £800 – and cost £36.

Secretaire-bookcases were normally made 3′ 9″ or 4′ 0″ wide and these are now considered too big. Reduced to 3′ 6″ they will fetch £350 or more. Most, however, undergo the following operation and become 'rather unusual' china-cabinets:

The secretaire drawer is removed, the dustboard beneath it, which is usually dovetailed to the sides and therefore expensive to remove, is left in place, but the two round holes through which you put your fingers to work the springed pieces of timber that control the secretaire drawer, are plugged and perhaps veneered over; then the bottom part of the bookcase is reduced in depth so that the doors of the top part are flush with those of the bottom part.

The evidence of this operation will be the plugged holes or else the veneered floor. Other evidence will be the low waist of the piece, inevitable because writing height is 2′ 6″, whereas the table top of a genuine china-cabinet would be 3′ 5″ from the ground.

Tallboys, being deep, take up too much space in our modern rooms and are not often bought except to turn into other things. One sold in November 1964 for £18 became a chest (the top part of the tallboy to which a flat top and set of four feet have been added) which I saw being offered for £145, and a 'rare commode' (the base of the tallboy with carved legs from two single chairs) was recently in a shop and priced at over £2,000.

The cupboard type of commode has always fetched high prices and many that you will see are conversions from side tables. Most side tables started life with four square tapered legs, the taper, of course, being on the inside. No old cabinet-maker would ever have fixed

4   Design for wardrobe.

Doors for Book-Cases &c

5 It is easy to doctor the doors of a wardrobe like that shown opposite to make them like those for 'bookcases etc.' in the drawing above and, if the depth of the top part is reduced, you have a fine and valuable piece worth four figures.

a door to a tapering leg (see *Hinges*), but that is what has to be done in this type of conversion and that always gives it away. One such side table, bought from a doctor in Hampstead for £140, was turned into a commode and at the time of writing was in an antique shop and priced at £3,750.

Other cupboard commodes are made from semi-circular ends of leg dining tables. With these, the doors always hang wrongly because the hinges have to be fixed to a tapering leg (see p. 57). But there is a further give-away in the fact that the height of a dining table being 28″ and that of a commode 36″, the legs have to be made higher. Six or seven inches are added to the bottom of the legs in what is called a 'bandage' (see *Bandage*).

In 1962 the end of a dining table was bought for £5 at a sale by a cabinet-maker who crossbanded the top and made it into a commode at a total cost of £53. Put in a London auction it fetched £850.

Most Chippendale desks sold in the last twenty years have been Victorian pieces which have had their rounded corners made square, their half-round mouldings on the top and plinth altered to a small ogee moulding and their drawers cockbeaded (see p. 47). One bought for £2·50 had work worth £40–£50 put in on it, was sold to an antique dealer for over £300 and to a member of the public for more than £600.

The smaller a desk is, the easier it is to sell and the higher the price you will obtain for it. The big 5′ 0″ × 3′ 9″ desks are some-times cut in half lengthwise and turned into not one, but two 'genuine' Chippendale desks by the treatment I have described. One treated in this way at a cost of £96 (for the

two) earned its converter £785: one being sold in a London auction while the other was sent to the north and there auctioned for over £400.

In the last twenty years more money has

6 This is the eighteenth-century wardrobe (see *graze marks*).

been made out of selling converted sofa-tables than out of any other single item of furniture. Sofa-tables are usually made from the end standard supports of period cheval mirrors, but they have even been made from dough troughs. When made from cheval mirror supports, the bar below the mirror has to be removed and often one of the uprights which held the mirror is put in its place; this puts the end supports the right distance apart to become a table with the addition of a top. However, in the middle of the upright there is a square part with a hole where the thumbscrew for tightening the mirror used to be; this hole has to be plugged and the traces covered, usually with a circular patera. As the part is square, four patera are normally used.

Tripod tables are made from pole fire-screens by removing the pole and banner and raising the stem of the tripod by nearly eight inches and then fitting a piecrust or similar tray on top. I remember one fire-screen on a nicely carved tripod fetching £10 at a London sale. A very good restorer added six inches of wood left over from the post of a four-poster, earlier turned into a pair of torchères, to the shaft and put on top a piecrust tray that cost him £3. The total cost of this 'reconstituted' tripod table was £19.50, yet a London dealer gave £650 for it. Other tripod tables are made from the poles of four-poster beds to which feet and tops are added. Four-poster poles also become torchères and candlesticks. The bed itself, if made of oak, can become a court cupboard or a small buffet (so can a refectory table). One William and Mary four-poster auctioned in London in 1937 was turned into a 3′ 9″-court cupboard and sold to a museum for £1,050.

7 How easy to turn 6 into this, the 'Secretaire Bookcase'.

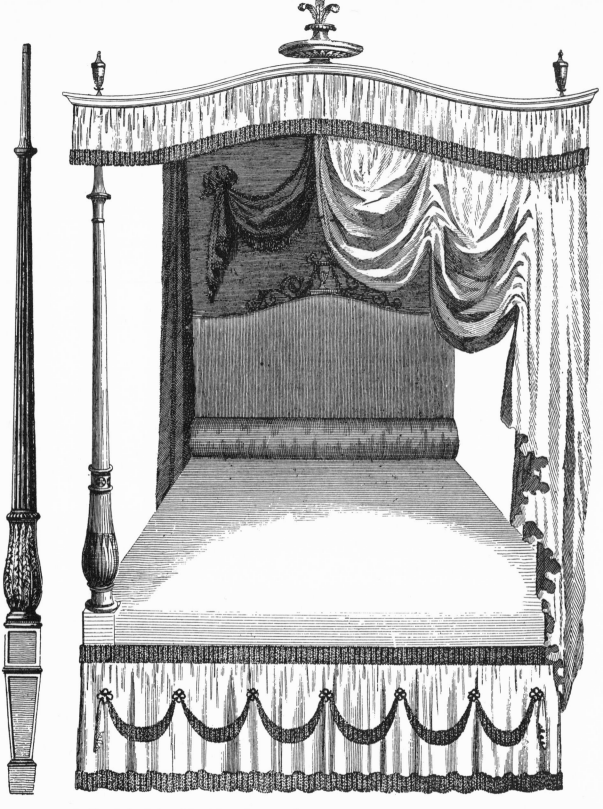

8 Here is the design of the eighteenth-century four-poster bed, and the design of the posts used. How easily these can become torchères, or candle stands is all too obvious or, an expensive tripod table.

It is simple to reduce a sideboard of any shape from, say, 6′ 0″ to 4′ 0″ and to do so without anybody knowing; but when the width of a piece is reduced, then its depth from front to back must also be reduced to keep the piece in proportion, and this it is impossible to disguise. In reducing a sideboard, first the top is unscrewed and the veneer steamed off it; then the top is cut right through the middle, lengthwise, giving two pieces; the piece with the back edge on it is left undisturbed, the requisite amount of the reduction being cut off the part with the front attached to it; the two pieces are then glued together and the veneer replaced. The drawers are dealt with in the way already explained (see p. 28) and the piece is ready. All sideboard tops must overhang a little at the back, front and sides, so, if you run a finger along the underside of the overhang you will feel a join – or a strip of veneer covering a join; even if the underside of the overhang has been veneered to cover up the join you will still be able to feel and see the join if you remove the drawers and look at or run your hand along the underside of the top. Don't accept it, if you are told that the timber has shrunk and caused the top to split, because if that had been the case, the veneer on the top would also have split.

The chiffonier is another article of furniture that fetches high prices today complete with wire-grilled doors and pleated silk panels. The cost of materials and labour for these chiffoniers can be £42·50 each, and dealers can pay £120–£165 at the auctions to which the first purchasers send them, believing them to be Regency.

Another source of 'naughty' pieces is the Victorian item that has had its horrors removed. In this way Victorian pedestal desks become Chippendale desks, Victorian drum tables are made into Sheraton drum tables, and mahogany hanging shelves are turned into Chippendale by having their sides fretted.

These are the main things that can and *are* done to convert furniture and to make it more saleable and acceptable to the public (or to deceive the public, if you are feeling uncharitable). Poor public!

Now when it comes to the point and you are considering buying a piece, how do you safeguard yourself? By remembering the above and properly vetting your piece.

In Part Five I shall deal with the individual types of furniture and explain the vetting necessary for each but Part Three describes the points to look at, the symptoms on which you will base your diagnosis and answer the question, is it genuine?

9, 10 Designs for bedposts.

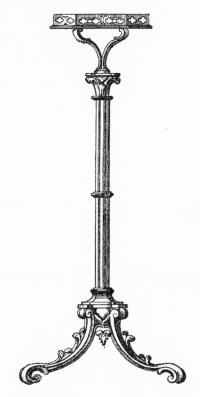

PART THREE

Where to Look and What to Look For

Apron

An apron is a structural part of furniture. In tables it is the piece connecting the legs, just under the top; in chairs it is beneath the seat; in cabinets, etc., it is along the base; it is also sometimes called a skirt.

To put an apron round the underside of a table top, especially of a circular table, was an idea of the Victorians, who thought it ought to stop the top warping – which it doesn't! These aprons were screwed onto the top and where they have been removed, as they sometimes are to 'destroy the evidence', you will find screw holes at intervals around the underside of the top, no doubt neatly plugged.

11 Here is a table with the apron in place. Note its platform base and ugly Victorian nulling.

Backs

The back is perhaps the most important thing to examine of all pieces that normally stand against a wall, for this is where the patination should be. The edges of the back-timbers should be black. It is at the back that you will see the tell-tale joins that show where timber has been added, the cuts where a piece has been removed etc. Marriages practically all give themselves away at the back. One could almost say that you should begin your vetting at the back. I know that people sometimes feel diffident about asking for a piece to be pulled away from the wall, especially if it is a heavy piece, but when a three- or four-figure sum is involved, why on earth should it not be done? It is important. *Always* look at the back.

12   Back of chest.

Bandage

A bandage consists of four pieces of veneer (or wood) put round the leg of a piece of furniture. It is used to hide a join made when the leg was extended in order to increase the height of the piece.

You do very occasionally find a bandage put onto the legs of a late Sheraton piece solely for decoration, but these pieces are rare, and, as a general rule, bandages are suspect. (See *Legs*.) Where a bandage is original and thus right, the grain of the timber will be the same on each side of the bandage, if it is not, then the bottom piece of the leg is an addition.

13a   Here is a rough bandage of moulding (Note how the grain (and timber) is different above and below the bandage).

13b   and this is what it hides.

Beading

Period beading, such as that illustrated, was carved out of wood and so the grain follows all the way through, or it should. Nowadays the beads are made of plaster of Paris and stuck on individually.

The beading on the edge of William IV tables (see *Nulling* p. 64) is now removed by the restorer and replaced by an ogee moulding.

14 Genuine eighteenth-century beading, all out of one piece of wood.

15 Victorian or Edwardian beading: the 'beads' are separate and just glued on.

Bearers

Genuine bearers supporting the top of a table were always tapered and ended so far from the end (or side) of the table that they could not be seen without bending down to look under the table. If you can see them without bending, as you can here, it shows that the ends have been cut to reduce the length, or even just to make a square end into a D-end.

When a table has been reduced in this way, the fact will often be obvious in that the distance between the pillars and the ends of the table looks, and is, too short relative to the size of the pedestals.

16 Table bearers.

Brass

Always look at the brass, for this is one of the most important means of identification. Remember that the cabinet-makers of the eighteenth century would not allow handles or escutcheons to detract from the beauty of the pieces. If, for instance, they were making a double-height piece, they would use escutcheons of the same size in both parts, and the smaller these were the better they liked them. Brass work was made by blacksmiths who were real craftsmen, for their locks and bolts still work perfectly after two hundred years of use. The old brass they used had a higher percentage of copper than that of today and in time it goes a green colour which no modern brass achieves.

Today, locks, handles, escutcheons, are, of course, still manufactured from the old designs as they have been for many years, but the brass used is modern and quite different in colour to that of eighteenth-century brass. The catalogues of the firms that make reproduction cabinet fittings for restorers and the makers of reproduction furniture show that there is little you cannot obtain: cabinet handles, drop, ring, lion-head and wine-cooler handles, lifting handles, escutcheons, wardrobe, pedestal and cupboard turns, hinges, bolts and castors (low, square, round socket, lion-claw and plain shoe), knobs, drops (Dutch, fancy, axe), glass screws, locks, tray handles, table catches, table clips, bed-post covers, astragal moulding, quadrant stays, desk galleries, spandrels, clock faces, pillar corners, Corinthian capitals, clock pillar bases, spires and eagles for clocks, lock-plates; mounts for cabinets of various kinds, shutter and drawer knobs. All these are made from the old designs, but the brass of which they are made will be different. That is your only safeguard, if you should come across any of them on a piece offered you as antique.

Castors

The early brass castors found on Chippendale had wheels made of three or four pieces of leather and the 'hub' fitted up into the leg.

17a   Chippendale brass castor.

17b   Bucket castor (The shaft of this has met with an accident and been twisted. Normally it would be straight.)

The bucket castor with brass wheel was introduced about 1760. Bucket castors of this type are manufactured today for reproduction furniture, but as with all other brass articles, the percentage of copper in the brass is not as high as it was in the eighteenth century and you do not get the same green shade.

17c Square box castor.

The square box castor was used on a square leg and is generally found on pieces made between 1760 and 1800.

Carving

Whether of a patera or on legs, backs, arms, etc. carving should always be above the surface of the rest of the timber and very bold. The eighteenth-century cabinet-maker did not have to economize with his timber, so he cut away and down into the timber he was carving, leaving the design standing up boldly on its own. Flat or countersunk carving must have been added at a later date. (You can even cut your hand feeling the knees of old chairs and settees, the carving is so crisp.) Around and in old carving there will always be patination.

Many 'Chippendale' chairs are in fact late Georgian ones which have been carved at a later stage and ruined in the process. Such carving is inevitably flat or countersunk.

The Victorians, who made endless copies of Chippendale, used larger chisels than those of the eighteenth-century workmen and these leave different marks. The Victorians also economized on timber, so that their carving is much flatter.

In 1952, a Georgian desk was carved for a dealer. This involved carving all the mouldings and the work, plus the cost of the desk and an old set of handles, cost £140. Today, the desk is in the home of a private collector who paid £3,500 for it.

A few years ago a breakfront-bookcase came on the market. It had been carved in 1963, when it had also had a new cornice made for it. When bought in the original state in 1960 it cost the dealer £350; in 1965, after treatment, it sold as Chippendale with original carving (and cornice) for nearly £6,000.

See also *Nulling*.

Chair-arms

All the best cabinet-makers had workshops in London and all London-made chairs had the arms put on from the side of the back leg. They were not fixed to the front of the back leg. This may be seen in a few country-made chairs, but these do not have the quality or the value of the London-made chair. (See also *Chairs*, p. 110)

18 Fine deep, sharp carving on a genuine George II chair.

Chair Top Rail

No chair was ever made with a top rail that overlapped the sides until 1840 and not in any numbers until 1850. The overlapping top rail is thus a sure sign of Victorian origin. In the genuine period chair the top rail must be contained within the two back legs, thus:

19   Chair top rail.

It is expensive to make an overlapping rail come within the two back legs, so the restorer will round the square corners of an overlapping rail and perhaps box in the round (turned) legs or add new legs.

If the legs are new you may be able to see a join or a line of inlay hiding a join, as the timber will be different.

Cock-beading

This is a narrow moulding, of semi-circular section, protruding round the front edges of a drawer. Nearly all drawers from 1720 to 1800 were finished in this way, the cock-beading being made of mostly walnut or mahogany.

The most important thing is that these cock-beads were always glued. If cock-beads have been pinned on (usually in three places) then I consider the piece was made either in Victorian times or later. Or it may have been clumsily mended.

20   Here is a typical cock-bead held by pins.

Cockleshell

The cockleshell was a favourite ornament of the Victorians, who even added it to eighteenth-century pieces no doubt increasing their attraction to themselves, but reducing their value to us. The presence of a cockleshell inlay on a piece thus means either that it is of Victorian manufacture, or is an embellishment added to a genuine piece at a later date. You should assume the former, until the latter can be proved.

Cross-Banding

A different timber (strip of veneer) glued around the top edge of a piece of furniture for ornament, or, in the case of a desk, as a frame for leather covering the top. It is also used round the edges of drawers, sometimes outside herringbone inlay lines. Wherever it is used, in this way, the grain of cross-banding should always be at right-angles to the direction of the herringbone inlay (see p. 58), i.e. the strip of veneer is cut across the grain. As with herringbone inlay, cross-banding that is absolutely flat is suspect, and may well have been added recently.

Doors

Single doors always open to the right (i.e. the lock or handle is on the left, the hinges on the right). Nothing was ever made for left-handed people.

When the old cabinet-makers made a panel door, they always chose their best figured timbers for the panel and when putting them in the frame used either an astragal moulding or inlaid lines. They always used a differently figured timber for the outer edge of the frame.

Later, when the eighteenth-century cabinet-maker made a piece with double doors, he put three hinges on each door (see *Hinges*) and, where the two doors met, a narrow, thin astragal moulding of wood or brass was screwed on, not pinned. This was to allow for the inevitable shrinkage of the timber of the doors and prevent a visible gap.

The Victorians with their grosser tastes made the moulding much wider.

Where there are double doors, one door is fitted with bolts top and bottom which, of course, are countersunk. These are always on the left-hand door.

21 Here is a genuine double-heighted piece where everything is right.

Double-heighted pieces

In these pieces the sides of both sections were always made from the same piece of timber as they were always of the same thickness, top and bottom. Grain and colour must thus be the same. Similarly the stiles of the doors were the same width in top and bottom sections.

With double-heighted pieces, always move the piece away from the wall to see the back edges of the side timbers which should be of the same thickness and the same colour. It is no good looking only at the sides, as, if the piece has been married, it will have had the sides re-veneered with the same veneer. But in a married piece, it is exceedingly unusual to find that both sections have side timbers of exactly the same thickness, as they would in a genuine double-heighted piece.

The back stretcher rail of a double-heighted piece (chest-on-stand etc.) was always made straight to provide the strength needed to help support the weight of the top piece.

Curved back stretcher rails were used only on low pieces.

The same kind and size of escutcheons were used in both sections.

Drawers

If you remove the drawers from a piece and turn the piece upside down, you should find that there are paler patches on the underside of the top, corresponding to the drawers.

When two drawers are side by side, they should be of the same size. No eighteenth-century drawer would fill completely the distance between front and back.

Sides

On all good quality drawers the sides will be of oak and the top edges of the sides will be rounded. The thinner the sides the better.

Bottom Boards

Up to 1770 the grain in the bottom boards of all drawers ran from front to back (after that date it ran from side to side). To allow for shrinkage, the eighteenth-century cabinet-maker made the bottom boards of his drawers in two or three pieces. In all genuine period drawers, the bottom and back boards are likely to be split in places where the timber has shrunk. From Victorian times the bottom board would be made in one piece, and screwed on, not nailed as in the earlier pieces.

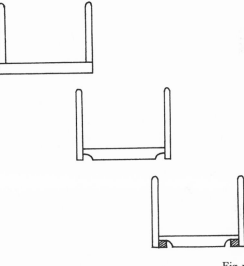

Fig 1

These diagrams are of sections showing different drawer constructions. In the earliest pieces (1) the bottom boards of drawers were used for drawers to run on. Later the oak drawer sides were made to pass the bottom board (2) and were used as drawer runners. (3) shows the commonest construction, where strips of wood are glued to the base as reinforcement to the runners.

 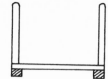

Fig 2

These are modern drawer constructions. If found on a piece purporting to be eighteenth-century, they are a clear give-away.

Here is the bottom board of an eighteenth-century drawer, showing the runner which is a strip of wood glued along the edge. It is a good example of the grain running from front to back. The side runner is worn as one would expect.

Mouldings

If a drawer has corner mouldings fixed inside and glued to both sides and bottom, the piece cannot be earlier than 1800, because corner mouldings were invented by Sheraton in 1799. Note that the corner mouldings in Sheraton pieces and those of the other late eighteenth-century cabinet-makers will be a hollow moulding but in Victorian times they were half-round mouldings.

Victorian Half Round

Fig 3

Sheraton Hollow Moulding

Fig 4

People used to fill drawers with things that were too heavy for them and so made the bottom board loose; the corner mouldings helped to stop this.

Dovetails

Obviously the two sides of each drawer must be made of the same timber and the dovetails must be the same (see *Desks, Knee-hole*). Any difference in the dovetails will indicate that the piece has been restored, converted or interfered with in some way.

All drawers, large and small, have a scribe mark to show where the dovetail ends. If a drawer has been reduced in depth it may have been cut through the scribe marks, the required amount taken off the sides and bottom board, and the two parts flimsily joined together again (see opposite). In that case the grain of the timber in the sides will not continue through the scribe marks (though marks

22 Note that this drawer is made from close-grain oak used in early pieces. If the grain is wide with black speckles like tadpoles, it is oak of a much later date, used on pieces of furniture made after about 1860.

In old furniture no drawer, large or small, ever ran the full depth of the piece; a gap of anything up to two inches was always left between the drawer and the back of the piece to allow air to circulate.

Inlay

On walnut pieces where the drawer fronts are finished with a herringbone inlay, this inlay should always run in a clockwise direction (see *Veneers*). If the herringbone is level or countersunk, the inlay has probably been laid recently, for genuine herringbone inlay will nearly always have risen in a few places (see *Inlay*).

All drawers should have handles.

Where a piece has drawers of different size, the smaller drawers are always above the larger.

Drawers in a piece with more than one layer of drawers must all be of the same width.

Veneer on the inside face of a drawer is a probable indication that old handle holes have had to be plugged and the plugs disguised, probably because the width of the drawer has been reduced.

Patination

Drawers should have patination on the sides where fingers touch as the drawer is pushed in and there should be the same amount on either side.

scratched with a pin can imitate grain very successfully). So always check this point carefully. If, when you pull out a drawer, you find that it is 'front-heavy', that is, inclined to fall out because of its own weight, you will know that the drawer was originally much bigger and had to have a stouter, heavier front than that needed for a drawer with the present dimensions.

23b The upper of these two drawers is a good example of a neat English dovetail (with scribe mark). The drawer beneath is a bad fake that was passed off as Sheraton. It has clumsy dovetailing and no scribe mark.

Number of drawers

Eighteenth-century cabinet-makers were rigid about the number of drawers that were included in the various pieces they made.

The *Bureau* had either two short and three long drawers, or four long drawers, or a dummy top drawer and three long drawers.

A *Bureau-bookcase* had, in the bureau part, either: two short and three long drawers or four long drawers; or a dummy top drawer and three long drawers.

A *Chest-of-drawers* had either two small and three long drawers or four long drawers.

A *Tallboy* had two or three short drawers and three long drawers in the top and three long drawers in the bottom part.

Escutcheons

The escutcheons used for each piece of furniture were identical in size, shape and design. They were always placed in the centre of the drawer or of the stile of the door (halfway between top and bottom), so that if they are not centred in this way, you can be sure that the piece has been tampered with. Genuine eighteenth-century escutcheons are rounded at the bottom (24a).

24a

24b

Those with square bottoms are Victorian (24b).

Georgian-shaped escutcheons are still made (see p. 44) for reproduction furniture, but they are always obvious imitation because of the colour of the brass of which they are made.

When there are doors or drawers in a line, the escutcheons will be in a line too. When you see pictures where this is not the case, they have probably been tampered with.

All eighteenth-century drawers had escutcheons in the middle. I have seen pieces with no escutcheons at all, as here,

25 Drawers without escutcheons.

but I would not accept them as eighteenth-century. In our period ivory escutcheons were used only on small objects like a tea caddy or a late Sheraton toilet mirror. They were never used on cabinet work until Victorian times. Ivory discolours fairly quickly so that a period ivory escutcheon would not show up 'brilliantly white' in a photograph.

Fret

The open fretwork on Chippendale furniture such as silver-tables and tripod-tables or on the front of shelves, called Chinese railing, though thin, was laminated and in section

26a Here is genuine fretwork topping a mahogany secretaire.

looks like three-ply. It was made in this manner for strength and to allow the timbers to breathe.

The thicker, open fretwork on the side of hanging bookshelves etc. must be of a different pattern between each shelf. Whether the fretwork is thick or thin, in genuine pieces of the period you never find two shelves one above the other with the same pattern.

There are designs in eighteenth-century drawing-books showing fretwork of the same pattern between each shelf. But these designs were not adopted by contemporary craftsmen, who soon discovered that fret was much stronger if the pattern was different between each shelf, and it became the rule that this should be so.

Fret was cut with a very thin round 'pencil' saw. This left all corners round. Chippendale insisted that all corners of his fret must be square, except in a design of curves, and they had to be squared off with a file.

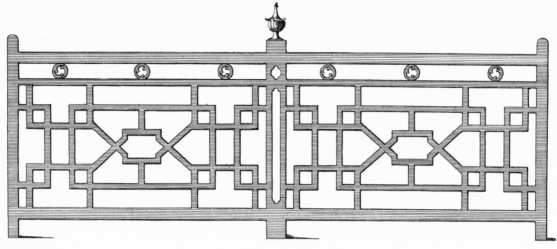

26b Here is one of the eighteenth-century square designs.

Where Victorian mahogany hanging-shelves have been subsequently fretted, as is done today, the saw marks will still be rough to the touch, whereas on eighteenth-century work, though the timber will still feel uneven, the surface will be smooth and slippery with patination.

Some 'naughty' chairs have square legs carved in the style of frets, and stretchers with fret piercing. This was very rarely done and is thus suspect.

Blind fret is fret on a solid ground, that is not pierced through.

Fronts

If the topboard of a piece of furniture is shaped (bow or serpentine) then the piece of timber on which it rests must be of the same shape.

Gilding

There were two methods of gilding; water gilding and oil gilding. Water gilding was the best and most expensive. Here, a thin skin of size and whiting was painted on the frame, then a paste of blue clay and parchment size was added in several coats; when this was dry, it was dampened and the gold leaf applied. Often as many as three layers of gold leaf were put on.

The other method, oil gilding, was cheaper. Here the frame was painted with gold size, then with oil, boiled with yellow colouring. When nearly dry, but still tacky, gold leaf was applied to this, but only in one layer.

Blue was the colour of water-gilding. *Yellow* the colour of oil-gilding.

The inner part of a frame will often get worn over the years with cleaning and the colour will peep through, revealing which method of gilding was used.

Red was never used until Victorian times, when gilders used deep colours to highlight the gold.

Glazing

Glazed doors are fitted with glass in panes, often fixed into a lattice pattern of woodwork of straight astragal bars.

Today, the cheapest way of glazing is to put one sheet of glass in the door and add fake astragal bars afterwards. The old and better way is for the astragal bars to be put in the frame of the door (remember that they must be dovetailed in) and the separate pieces of glass inserted and fixed with putty afterwards.

Remember that putty mixed with plaster of Paris and dust will dry hard and dirty in seconds, so that there is not necessarily any justification for the assertion, often made in shops, that because the putty is as hard as rock, it must be original.

Glass panes in a door that have been *in situ* for 150 years or more tend to 'warp' and should have a slight outward curve.

same way as that of the timber beneath, whichever direction that happened to be. The Victorians thought that having the grains running counter to each other would stop warping; they were wrong. Sheraton also used the later method for the veneered tops of some pieces. As a result of changes in temperature and humidity, veneer put on in this way will have buckled or warped, and probably therefore been replaced.

On Queen Anne pieces, the veneers on flat surfaces, such as chest tops and drawer fronts were always quartered.

Where there are inlaid lines on a piece, the grain of the veneer should never continue through the lines of inlay. If it does, it means that the inlay is a later addition (see *Inlay*).

Grain

Always look closely at the grain of timber, both of the veneers and the carcase of a piece. Very open or heavily-marked grain in veneers are often suspect (see *Inlay* and *Veneer*).

In pieces such as bureau-bookcases, secretaire-bookcases, china-cabinets and tallboys, the grain of the timber used for the sides of both sections should be the same (see *Double-Heighted Pieces*).

On tripod furniture, particularly small tripod tables which are rare and therefore often made up, make sure that the grain of the timber runs through the full length of the pole (see *Tripods*).

The grain of the timber used for the bottom boards of drawers should run from front to back (see *Drawers*). Check the drawer sides: the grain of the wood should continue through the scribe marks. Any break in grain here would indicate that the drawer has been reduced in depth (see p. 51 and *Drawers*).

In the eighteenth century and earlier, veneer was applied so that the grain ran the

Graze Marks

Where a wardrobe had tray-shelves, which pulled out, these almost always left graze marks on the inside of the doors, caused by the shelves being pulled out when the doors were not open wide enough and thus catching on them. Many a china-cabinet or other piece converted from such a wardrobe still has the marks on the inside of its doors, now in all probability glazed. Their presence is proof enough of the piece's origins.

Similarly, people usually leave the keys in the doors of bookcases, china-cabinets etc. In a large piece, where a door opens within the width of the piece, the key in the key hole is likely to bump against the stile or another part and there will be a graze mark in this place. If a piece has graze marks in one part but not in another, where you would expect to find them, it is an indication that the piece is composite and not as originally designed.

Grilles

The wire grilles on eighteenth-century doors are made of brass and where wires cross, one is notched to take the other, leaving the surface of the join flat.

27a   Wire grilles.

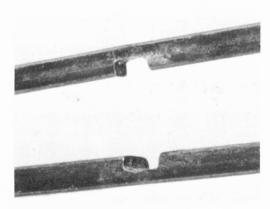

27b   Wire grilles showing notches.

In Victorian grilles not only is the brass of a different colour, but the wires cross one over the other without interlocking (i.e. there are no notches) and a stud is soldered on to hide the join. There are no studs on eighteenth-century grilles.

Handles

The handle itself, pummel plate, pummel pin and nut were always made of brass. Threads were cut by hand and the pummel pins were not pointed. The nuts had a notch cut in either side and were tightened with a special spanner that fitted into these notches (28).

Whether in pedestal-desk, tallboy, chest, or anything else, the handles of all drawers etc. must be in line. If they are not, the piece has been tampered with.

28

Handles should be in the centre of the drawer and in proportion to the drawer they are on. Where they are far up the drawer or where they hang down too far towards the bottom of the drawer, or even below it, in one extreme case I have seen, it is a sure sign that the drawers (and the piece) have been tampered with.

Hinges

The only articles of eighteenth-century furniture in which the hinges can be seen when looked at from in front are the corner-cupboard, the bedside commode and the grandfather clock. On all other pieces the doors were hinged onto the face of the side timbers, so that only the knuckle of the hinge can be seen and then only when looked at from the side.

On William and Mary or Queen Anne pieces with heavy panelled or mirrored doors, pin-hinges were always used as they are very strong. A pin-hinge consists of strips of brass countersunk into and screwed to the top and bottom edges of the door; at the outer ends of these strips are protruding pins which fit into matching holes in the similar strips of brass screwed to the underside of the cornice and the top of the base. Pin-hinges continued to be used throughout the eighteenth century on commode doors where ordinary hinges would show from the front. The disadvantage of this type of hinge is that if it becomes damaged it is not easily replaced, as either the top of the piece or the cornice has to be taken off.

Chippendale started the custom of using three hinges on the top doors of his double-heighted pieces. From his time onwards, the top sections of all genuine eighteenth-century pieces have three hinges, as on the door shown here (29a).

No eighteenth-century craftsmen ever put a hinge on a tapered leg, but you will see it done on second-rate conversions. It looks wrong and it is wrong.

29a

29b Here is a genuine piece with pin-type hinges. (Note, too, how the grain is different on either side of the inlaid lines, as it should be.)

30a   And here is a piece which suggests that the inlay has been added at a later date (grain continuing through the inlay).

Inlay

Eighteenth-century inlay has different timbers on either side of the inlaid lines; thus if the grain continues past an inlaid line, the inlay cannot be original.

On the tops and drawer fronts of early eighteenth-century walnut pieces, where the veneer is quartered, there is always a herringbone inlay running clockwise round the quartering. The herringbone is made of two pieces of veneer running side by side and looks like a chevron with the grain running slantwise. It should be possible to feel the dividing line between the central quartered veneer and the herringbone inlay, as shrinkage over the years will have forced the inlay up a fraction. If the inlay is countersunk or level with the rest of the veneer, it is probably a recent addition.

Decorative inlay is often added to, say, the two ends of a dining table (worth £18) to make them a pair of side tables worth £500 at least. Before the plain table surface can be inlaid it has to be scraped (removing about 1/16th inch) thus all the old patination and polish goes and the grain is left as open as when the timber was first planed. To close it as before will take a couple of centuries and so the grain of the side tables gives them away.

Eighteenth-century inlay must by now have been forced up in places, owing to the main timber shrinking. If inlaid lines are countersunk or even everywhere level with the main surface, they will be recent additions.

Remember that in the chevron or herringbone effect of the feather banding, mostly used on Queen Anne walnut (flat surfaces), the points of the 'arrows' must go clockwise.

Keys

Eighteenth-century keys are made of steel and have bow-shaped handles. The thinner the bow, the more likely it is to be old.

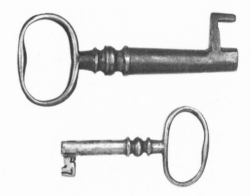

31   Eighteenth-century keys.

30b   Top: feather banding.

Legs

If a piece of furniture has square tapered legs, only the inside of the legs is tapered; the outside edge of the legs is perfectly square.

Legs are always made of one piece of timber and in the case of sideboards, etc. should run from the top board right down to the floor. In many sideboards the grain of the timber in the legs changes where the main body of the piece begins, showing that the leg does not continue to the top board, as it should if this piece had been genuine.

A bandaged leg is suspect, especially if the bandage is high up, as it often means that the leg has had a piece added to it to make it the right height for the use to which it is being converted.

Crab-type legs such as you can see on pedestal dining-tables (and other pedestal pieces) are a Victorian weight-carrying invention.

32   A Victorian table with crab-type tripods.

Circular Victorian legs are often converted into eighteenth-century ones by turning them to half their width, then boxing them in with four pieces of thick veneer. The finished product is tapered on the inside, which, of course, makes it appear eighteenth-century. What will give it away, as well as an inevitable slight difference in colour from that of the rest of the piece, is the bottom of the leg. This will either have a box castor (which would have to be removed to reveal the naughtiness, but only

the best restorers would go to the expense of this), or it will be veneered, which must strike everyone as extraordinary, or it will have a dome of silence. Remove this (or the box castor) and this is what you will see:

One side of the round leg has been flattened to produce the requisite taper (on the inside of the leg) and the whole then boxed in with four pieces of, in this case hardboard, but the faker would, of course, use veneer.

33 This is a rather crude 'mock-up' of what is done.

Locks

None of the old locks or door-bolts is stamped with a name or patent number; that did not come until Victorian times, so, if you notice the marks of a file or emery wheel on one side of the levers, you can be sure that the lock once had a name or patent number there, which has been filed away. With these old

eighteenth-century locks and door-bolts the cases will be of brass, but the actual levers and bolts will be of steel and either square or oblong. Victorian bolts have a circular shaft. Bramah locks and button-type escutcheons are Victorian. They were first made in large quantities in 1846 and remained popular for a

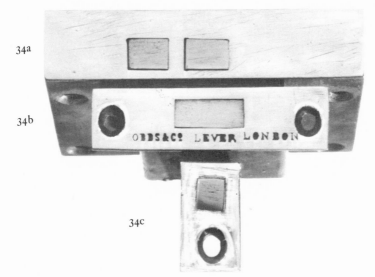

34a

34b

OBBS&C? LEVER LONBON

34c

long time. With these locks all that you see is a neat brass button with a small key hole in it, as in the drawers in the round table below. This was more obtrusive than the small key-shaped escutcheon, but because the Bramah

lock was burglar-proof it was often preferred by the Victorians. Some were added to eighteenth-century pieces, which, of course, reduces their value today.

35a Bramah locks.

Marble

White marble tops were widely used in Victoria's reign, so *white* marble tops on supposedly eighteenth-century pieces are suspect.

Genuine eighteenth-century marble can be red, pinkish, green, red mottled – almost any colour but white.

Marriage

A marriage is a naughty union of two pieces not made for each other to produce a double-heighted piece.

You will find many references to marriages in the text of this book.

They are indicated in many ways: by having two hinges instead of three on the

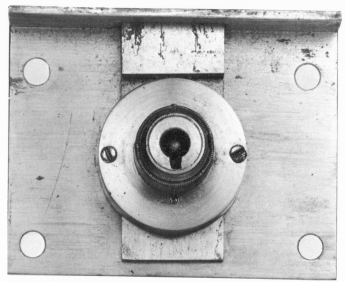

35b Behind the button, which is all you see on the surface, is a lock like
this, let into the back of the drawer or door in the normal way.

doors of the top part, or by having different escutcheons on the two parts. Often the bottom stretcher rail is curved, as for a single piece, instead of straight as is necessary to carry the weight of the double-heighted piece.

Always look at the back of any suspected marriage, where differences in patination, timber thickness etc. will be most evident.

Measurements

Here are the basic measurements, any substantial departure from which makes a piece immediately suspect.

BOOKCASES
The height is always greater than the width: you never find a bookcase, for example, that is 8′ 0″ wide by 8′ 0″ high.

SECRETAIRE-BOOKCASES
Width 3′ 9″ to 4′ 0″

BUREAUX
Width 3′ 0″ to 4′ 0″

CHAIRS
Seat of a single chair
Width 1′ 8″ to 1′ 10″

Seat of an arm chair
Width 1′ 10½″ to 2′ 2″
Height of all chair seat furniture from floor to top of seat 1′ 6″

CHESTS
Bachelor chest with fold-over top
Width 2′ 6″; depth 10″
Queen Anne chest-of-drawers
Width 2′ 6″; depth 1′ 8″

CHINA-CABINETS
Height of table top 3′ 5″

DESKS
Width 5′ 0″; depth 3′ 9″
Kneehole-desk or writing table:
Height from floor to top of space for knees 2′ 0″

TABLES
Dining table
Height 2′ 4″; width at least 4′ 0″ and up to 6′ 0″
Side table
Height 2′ 7″ and up to 2′ 11″

WRITING HEIGHT
Height 2′ 6″ to 2′ 8″

There may be some difference in dimensions of pieces that were specially made for a particular position; but the proportions would remain the same as those given here. So if a piece looks right and all the details are correct, it is probably genuine even if unusually large. If a piece *looks* wrong, check it very carefully indeed: the 'unusually small chest', the 'exceptionally slender bookcase' and so on, are all suspect.

Mouldings

A shaped profile applied to a continuous member to emphasize the difference in planes or to provide decorated bands of light and shade. Any break in a continuous flat surface may be considered a moulding if it is designed to catch the light and shade as an accent or embellishment. Certain general types of mouldings have been in use since the earliest architectural decoration. These are broadly classified as (1) flat or angular (2) single curved (3) compound curves. All types are variously embellished. The flat or angular types include (1) the band, face, or facia, continuous flat members, raised or sunken into and parallel with the main surface (2) the fillet, listel, or regula, a narrow band, usually projecting (3) the chamfer or bevel, an inclined band (4) the splay, a large bevel. The simple curved mouldings are (1) the cavetto, a concave moulding of a quarter circle, though the section may be flatter or more elliptical (2) Ovolo, the reverse of the cavetto, a convex quarter circle or flattened shape (3) the Flute, a semicircular groove which may be flatter (4) the Torus, a convex bulging shape of approximately a half circle (5) the Astragal, a small torus or bead (6) the Scotia, a hollow moulding of more than the quarter circle of the cavetto (7) the Roll Moulding, about three-quarters of a circle.

The Compound Mouldings are (1) the Cyma Rector (2) the Cymatium (3) Cyma Reversa, or Ogee, all serpentine or double mouldings, and (4) the Beak Mould, with the upper part concave and the lower convex.

Nails

If the back of the top of a double-heighted piece is nailed, so, too, will the back of the bottom part be nailed. Around the head of each eighteenth-century nail there will now be a dark stain in the wood, because differences in temperature and humidity in rooms will have caused the head of the nail to rust. In the making of many fakes, rusty nails are deliberately used, but they have not had time to stain the wood around them. The same thing applies to screws.

36a   Here is a fake drawer made with old rusty nails which, being rusty before they were driven in, have not stained the wood.

36b   Here is a genuine old piece of nailed wood showing the stains caused by the rusting of the nails (which have since been drawn).

Nulling

Nulling is ornamental carving consisting of convex curves, either straight or slanting, similar to quadrooning. Mostly seen on Victorian furniture, the larger and uglier, the later it is.

On a lot of Edwardian tables you find carved nulling on the edges of tops and bases. When the nulling runs differently top and bottom, say the bottom running) and the top (, I would think the top nulling was an addition to a tripod not originally made for a table.

Overhang

Look at the overhang of the tops of pieces. If it is more than one inch on each side, the top may well not belong to the rest of the piece.

All pieces made to stand against a wall had an overhang at the back of at least 2″ to allow for the skirting board.

No chair was made with a top rail that overhung the sides until 1840, and they were not made in any number until 1850 (see *Chair – Top Rail*).

Sideboards and side tables that started life 6′ 0″ long are often reduced to 4′ 0″ or 4′ 6″. If they are bow-fronted or serpentine-fronted, rather than lose too much of the shape, a large overhang is left on the top board, sometimes as much as 4½″ on each side. The presence of an overhang of this size is pretty conclusive evidence that the piece has been interfered with.

Patera

A patera is an ornamental round or oval carving in bas-relief. It was the 'trade-mark' of George Hepplewhite and should be carved out of the actual timber of the piece. Naughty

37 Straight nulling as on this table pedestal is Victorian. The straight bottom of the escutcheons also shows that the table is not eighteenth-century, but Victorian.

pieces often have paterae that have been applied later and either glued or nailed on, as was the one illustrated opposite.

Patination

Patination is probably the most important sign of the genuineness of antiques. It cannot be satisfactorily faked.

Patination consists of the dark patches of various size that you see on the backs, undersides, etc. of old pieces and around or in carving, places, in other words, which are either not usually dusted or polished, or are difficult to reach. Patination is dirt that has got into the grain of the wood over the years, as differences of temperature and humidity have caused it to open and shut. Dirt settles on the back and side edges that go against

38 Note the open grain of this patera.

walls and these eventually get quite black. Similarly, wherever fingers touch, the moisture that the skin deposits on the surface causes dust to adhere and this gets into the grain even when the surface is polished. Patination is mostly on the undersides of tables, chair arms, etc. where people's fingers clasp in order to lift or move the piece in question. It is also around handles and knobs of pieces that pull open and are pushed shut. Pieces that do not have patination where they should are either not genuine, have been tampered with, or have been repolished. More and more frequently, furniture sold in the antique dealers' shops has been repolished. It has the advantage that where a piece has been put together or converted, re-polishing will remove the evidence that lies in differences in the extent or depth of patination on timbers of different ages, and in the absence of patination where it should be. By thus restoring a piece to 'mint' condition, that of a piece leaving a cabinet-maker's workshop, you remove the one evidence of two hundred years of existence and use that no one can fake.

That it should be done to a genuine piece is to my mind incredible, but it is done.

When drawers are kept shut, perhaps locked, and the front is polished, some of the polish will spread inwards onto the top of the drawer front and the lock. This polish can only be rubbed if the polisher opens the drawer especially for this purpose; but in the great majority of cases this is not done and thus you will find that many eighteenth-century locks are quite dark with thick patination on top.

Similarly, polish gets into the crack where doors are hinged onto the sides and is not rubbed off in polishing. This again causes patination, which you should be able to see when the doors are open.

Again, when a chair has an open back, the perfect parlour maid would insert her cloth between the splats after applying polish and polish off the sides and bottom, but nine times out of ten, the cloth would miss out the top. Look for patination there.

Patination will be found round all handles.

Patination is very difficult to photograph

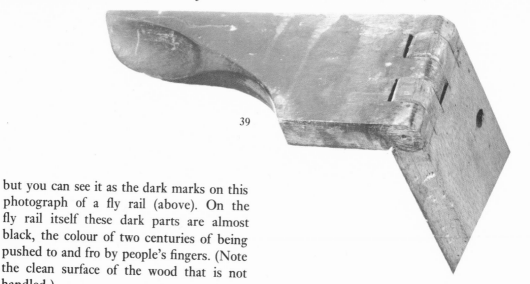

39

but you can see it as the dark marks on this photograph of a fly rail (above). On the fly rail itself these dark parts are almost black, the colour of two centuries of being pushed to and fro by people's fingers. (Note the clean surface of the wood that is not handled.)

Patination is your main guide to age and genuineness. Look for it in the following places:

1. On the front or the sides of drawers, especially if the drawers are large, as most people pull a long drawer open by the handles, but push it back by holding the front edges and the front part of the sides.
2. Under table tops and under the arms and seats of chairs.
3. On the back and side edges of pieces that stand against walls.
4. On all lopers, fly-rails and any parts that are handled.
5. On the under surfaces of galleries, etc., on desks and other pieces with little compartments.
6. On the hidden and unpolished side surfaces of legs, cornices, open-work chair backs, etc.

Pedestals

Pedestals supporting a period dining or other table ought to have four legs, not three. (See p. 133.)

Platform-Bases

Platform-bases were a Victorian fashion. There were, however, plinths on court cupboards, generally made of oak, but they come before our period. Nowadays almost everything on a platform-base is described as Regency, but apart from the base itself there are usually other details which will give away the true date.

Polish

Wax polishing is a lengthy and thus expensive business. French polishing, which involves filling up the grain with plaster of Paris to provide the polishing surface and then, with a pad, applying several films of dissolved shellac, is very much quicker and thus cheaper, for which reason the Victorians preferred it, after its introduction about 1861. French polish gives itself away because after a while the shellac wears off and the white of the plaster of Paris comes through, and you get a speckled effect, as shown in Plate 40.

40   A piece of banding that has been French polished.
(Magnified). You get exactly the same effect on a table
or any other piece.

Proportions

It is in the proportions that most of those who
tamper with and remake furniture go wrong.
The eighteenth-century designers were artists
and nothing they did was ever out of proportion. Your eye will usually tell you when
the proportions of a piece are wrong and a
tape-measure will confirm it.

You will often see the hood of a grandfather clock that does not belong to the case.
This will be shown by differences in thickness of the cornice and the plinth of the base,
which ought to be in proportion.

I have seen a kneehole-desk, where the top
of the kneehole came only half way up my
shin. It was an obvious fake.

Feet often reveal tampering. When a piece
is reduced the feet are often left untouched so
that, after the operation, they look heavier or
wider than the size of the piece justifies.
Trust your eye.

If the timbers used for the top, or sides, of
any pieces, appear unnecessarily thick, the
probability is that the piece has been cut down
to make it smaller and more acceptable.

Screws

Eighteenth-century screws were *not* pointed.
The first pointed screw was made by Nettle-
fold and shown at the 1851 Exhibition. They
were not mass-produced until a few years
later. Nowadays the faker will cut the point
off his screws in an attempt to make them
look pre-1851, but a mass-produced screw
can never look like the handmade article.

Screws, like nails, rust with differences in
temperature and humidity in rooms, and by
now eighteenth-century screw heads will have
stained the wood round them.

If screws were used to fasten the back of
one part of a double-height piece, they would
also have been used to fasten the back of the
other part as well; if not, beware! – it is a
marriage.

You can cut the end off a pointed screw,
but you cannot fake the black surface of the
old round-ended, eighteenth-century screw.

About 1870 many cabinet-makers dipped
their screws in glue before screwing them; so
if you experience difficulty in unscrewing a
screw, try heating the tip of your screwdriver

41a & b Eighteenth-century screw and thumb-screw.
41c Victorian (pointed) thumb-screw.

and letting it rest on the head for a few seconds. If that does the trick, it will also date your piece.

Screw-holes

Look high up on the inside of the sides of a two-heighted piece and if you see on each, two or three small holes that have been plugged, you will know that a socket for a rail was once fixed there and that the piece started life as a wardrobe.

Similarly, the presence of plugged screw-holes on the underside of a circular table almost certainly shows that the table once had aprons and so must have been made in Victorian days.

Seat-Rail

All seat furniture (chairs, settees, and stools) should measure 1′6″ from the ground to the top of the upholstery of the seat, whether it has a stuff-over seat or a drop-in seat. The seat-rails (the four rails the upholstery rests on) are normally 4″ deep. If a drop-in seated chair has deep seat-rails, then it is almost certain that the chair started life as a commode chair with a chamber-pot under the upholstered seat. The depth to the slats the pot stood on was generally 1′0″ or 1′2″ and so the seat-rails were made as much as 10″ deep, instead of the usual 4″, so as to hide most of this white china pot. As a commode chair can be bought very cheaply, but is nearly unsaleable, a dealer will shorten the seat-rails and make it saleable. The seat-rails cannot be shortened to the normal 4″, because the bottom edge of the seat-rails has to be retained to make the chair look genuine; but as the seat-rails on a commode chair have a deep apron made much lower in the centre (to hide as much of the pot as possible), the bottom part of the shaped seat-rail has to be retained and, unless it is going to look all out of proportion, the centre of the rail has to be much deeper than the normal four inches.

Hepplewhite made his front seat-rails of laminated wood to give them extra strength (he also did this on the front of side tables).

If a chair has different seat-rails it will probably have started life as a settee. Always remove hessian if there is any underneath, as this is often used to hide faults.

Shelf-Supports

In the eighteenth century shelves were supported by being fitted into grooves cut in each side of the cabinet, bookcase, etc., they were never balanced on pegs in holes.

Peg supports for shelves came late. They are William IV or more probably Victorian; but here again the holes for the pegs are made in the side of cabinet, not in the back, about $1\frac{1}{2}''$ from the front or back, while the shelves have notches cut out of the underside into which the pegs fit and in which they are hidden. Where there are grooves for shelves, these were cut on the inside of the side timbers before the piece was assembled. There must be equal space below the bottom groove and above the top one. Any discrepancy will mean that the piece has been tampered with, in all probability cut down from a larger one.

Stretcher-Rail

The centre stretcher-rails of all chairs, settees and stools (Chippendale, Sheraton or Hepplewhite) were dovetailed into the side-rails, so that when removed, the end of the stretcher-rail should look like this (42).

42   Stretcher-rail with dovetail.

Stretcher-rails should be about $4''$ off the ground; anything below this will suggest that the legs have been cut.

The back stretcher-rail of double-heighted pieces was always straight for strength, never curved. A curved stretcher-rail was used only on single-height pieces.

Timber

(For descriptions of the various woods used in eighteenth-century cabinet-making, see *Glossary of Timbers*, pp. 153-6.)

The eighteenth-century cabinet-maker did not start work unless he was sure he had enough timber to make the entire piece he was planning out of the same timber: sides, top, doors, drawers, etc.

There was no difficulty here, especially where mahogany was concerned. The resources of the West Indies and Central America had only just begun to be exploited and naturally, the huge old trees were felled first. They provided timber enough to make the largest dining table in one piece. The cabinet-maker had only to go down to the West India docks and choose his timber, selecting that with the grain he liked best. Mahogany was very expensive, even at the docks, but he would get his money back plus a handsome profit, when the piece was sold.

If it was a double-heighted piece he planned, he would use the same timber on the sides of both sections and they would be of the same thickness. Similarly, the stiles of the doors in the top and bottom (if there were any) would be of the same thickness. Thus when the sides of the top and bottom parts of a double-heighted piece are made of different timbers, or are of different thicknesses, it is a sure sign that they were not originally made for each other. The same is true if the fronts of drawers etc. are of different timber.

In the eighteenth century no one scamped his materials. The good cabinet-maker's pieces fetched a good price and so he bought ample material and if he planned carving, he allowed ample thickness and was quite prepared to cut all the rest of the wood away, so that the carving stood out free. The eighteenth-century cabinet-maker never 'made do' over materials, skill or anything else. He was a bit of a perfectionist and his customer expected near perfection from him.

Tool Marks

Where the marks of saw, chisel, etc. on the underside of the legs of tripods or of fretwork are clearly visible or feel rough to the touch, it means that the piece is of comparatively recent make. Even on undersides, eighteenth-century tool marks become covered with patination and so, though still uneven to the touch, the fingers will slide smoothly and easily over them; also they will not be readily visible.

The solid sides of wall shelves were sometimes fretted at a later date to make them look lighter; and many chairs with a solid wooden splat at the back have had this open fret cut. It is advisable when buying such pieces to do so in daylight; if you look at the fretting in daylight and see distinct tool marks, you know it cannot be an eighteenth-century chair (although of course the piece itself may be). When I buy a chair which has an open fret splat, I always turn the chair upside down so that I can see the amount of patination that has accumulated. When a chair stands on its legs, whoever dusts or waxes it will poke their fingers through the openwork that shows, but will forget to run the duster up to the top, and the amount of patination can be an eighth of an inch thick. (See also *Fret*.)

Tops

All eighteenth-century pieces with solid tops, no matter what size or shape, had tops cut from one piece of timber. This might be cut across subsequently to accommodate wings for Pembroke tables, etc., but the whole top will have been made from one piece of timber. It was only in Victorian times (from 1860 on) that people started making tops in two or three pieces, so as to allow movement in case the timber shrank.

By now, the solid tops of all eighteenth-century tripod circular tables have shrunk and if you measure them from north to south and from east to west, you will find a difference of at least half an inch. It is really only the circular tops that shrink so much.

If a top appears unduly thick it probably means that the piece has been reduced or else that the top is not the piece's original one.

Always look under the top board or boards and if there are any holes with no obvious justification, the top will have come from something else; also, where a table top tips up, the part that rests on the block should be lighter in colour than the rest of the underside which has been exposed to the air. When you remove any drawer from a piece and turn the piece upside down, you will find that the area of the underside above the drawers is lighter in colour than the rest.

Where the top was veneered, the veneer was in one piece, unless finished with cross-banding (see p. 58) or quartered (Queen Anne).

Sheraton used to make the grain of the veneer of the top run the opposite way to that of the timber underneath. Under the strains of changes in temperature and humidity, the two pull against each other and, as a result, the top buckles or warps. Where the pieces are in normal use, many of these tops have had to be replaced and you very seldom come across a period piece with a top that is buckled.

Tripods

If you buy *any tripod furniture*, lay the shaft across the palms of both your hands and turn the piece slowly looking along the shaft. It should be made of one piece of timber from beneath the top to between the three legs. If you look for the grain of the timber and follow it right along the shaft, it will be easy to spot a fake. Most fakers will insert a piece of timber to make a tripod higher from the nulling (the carved bulbous section or just a ring) so you must look very closely at these sections to make sure the timber grain runs through them. A very good tip is to put your warm hand round a section you are not sure about and you often find you can turn the shaft, when the warmth of your hand has melted the glue joining the section which has been added. Only a little glue is used; otherwise, when a piece is glued and then clamped together, the spare glue will be forced out and will have to be wiped away with a hot, wet rag and that leaves a tell-tale mark. Recently, I saw such a table priced at £850, which the seller insisted was genuine. I stood it near a radiator for a few moments and was then able to unscrew the stem in three places.

Veneers

Old veneers are thick, sometimes as much as an eighth of an inch. Later veneers are often wafer thin. This saved money. On the flat surface of Queen Anne pieces the veneers were quartered, with a herringbone inlay running clockwise round the edges. If the grain of veneer is particularly open, especially an inlaid piece, it may mean that the inlay is a later addition (see *Inlay*). Heavily marked walnut veneer is also suspect: in two hundred years black streaks would have faded or even disappeared.

43a   Eighteenth-century veneer.

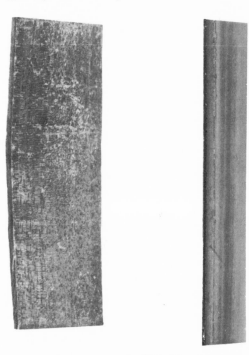

43b   Thin Victorian veneer.

PART FOUR

Birth of an Antique

This chest of drawers is a Victorian copy of a
Sheraton design. Several years ago it was sold
to a lady in London as genuine Sheraton, circa
1785, despite the fact that the moulding was
pure Victorian. It probably did not start life
with the Bramah locks that can be seen in
the photograph, but it is not known when
these were added. When bought in 1969, the

chest was in rather a poor state, especially the top, as can be seen from this second photograph. You will see that the second dustboard down on the left of the blocks on which the drawers ran, shows considerable wear and thus reasonable age. It was a well-made piece and thus lent itself to 'reduction' in the way described on page 84, and it was decided to turn it into one of the small chests that are usually described as 'unusual'. This is how it was done.

First the Victorian moulding was removed
and scrapped. It would not be wanted again.

Next the back had to come off. You can see
from this photograph that the left-hand
panel of the back was old and black with
patination, while the right-hand board had

been damaged and repaired. All the boards
had shrunk and the gap between the two side
boards and the centre board had been covered
over with paper, which left a white mark when
this was stripped off.

In this photograph showing the back removed, you can see how the drawers do not go right to the back, but leave a space of an inch and a half or so for ventilation. This is as it should be.

The next step was to remove the top. This was done by tapping from underneath with a hammer, undoing the dovetailing in this manner, and as the top came away it looked like this.

The curved board at the bottom in front had to be cut through in the middle and the requisite amount removed at that point. To have cut it off each side would have reduced the upward curve, making the line flatter and the appearance less pleasing.

This being a bow-fronted chest, the fronts of the dust boards between the drawers were made of a separate piece of curved wood and this was now tapped out with a hammer. These fronts are important pieces and have to be handled with care.

Next the dustboards themselves could be withdrawn from their grooved supports, and the process made the whole chest in a 'state of collapse': thus the reduction could now begin. This involved reducing the area of the dust boards to the required size, which had been settled beforehand, the curved fronts of these boards had then to be reduced in width and this was done very simply with a tenon saw. It was a simple matter to cut the sides through the middle and remove the necessary inches.

It had been decided to scrap the two small drawers at the top, as it would have involved a lot of extra time (and expense) to reduce them. Thus the curved front with the centre support, seen in the background of this picture, was scrapped.

The top had then to be cut, which was done quite simply with a band saw, only here the measurements were such as to leave enough wood overlapping at the sides and front to provide a 'moulding' for the top, of which more later.

In all these reductions it is the drawers that involve the most work. Here the dovetails joining the fronts and backs to the sides have to be tapped out, after which the curved fronts are cut to the required width thus.

The fronts then have new dovetails cut at either side. The sides of each drawer then have the dovetails cut off the front together with the amount of timber needed to reduce the side to the required length, and new dovetails are then cut in them. The backs of the drawers are then similarly reduced from one side and new dovetails cut.

When the width of a drawer is being left intact and only the depth is being reduced, a cruder but much quicker method of procedure is to saw through the scribe mark at the side of the drawers leaving the dovetail intact. When the sides have been reduced the requisite amount, they are fixed back on to the front with ordinary panel pins, the presence of which is hidden by the veneer, which is either the original that has been steamed off and replaced, or is entirely new.

In the case of these drawers, which were being reduced both in width and depth, this procedure was not practicable.

The handles on the drawers were rather ugly and it was decided to replace them with something that was more 'period'. It is, as has been said, possible to remove the veneer and re-use it, but in this case this would have involved plugging the holes where the handles had been and covering them with a matching piece of veneer, so it was decided to re-veneer the fronts of the drawers.

Veneer can either be steamed off, which is a simple though fairly lengthy process, or it can be removed with a blow-lamp, a method which is much quicker. The blow-lamp method is rather drastic, but you can re-use veneer removed in this way, providing you first scrape the varnish off it and are then careful not to scorch the veneer itself. When you play the flame of the blow-lamp on the veneer, the latter soon begins to buckle and you can get a knife or even your hand underneath and the whole thing will come away, as can be seen above.

All the other drawers were treated in the same way and after that it only remained to give the top its 'moulding', and the piece could be re-assembled.

It was decided that a nice reeded moulding would be suitably 'period', and it was demonstrated how this could quickly be provided using a special tool. The tool is one made in the workshop and consists of teeth from a broken band saw mounted in a wooden handle. With a quick firm action you scrape the teeth along the front of the timber and in no time at all you have a very convincing reeded moulding which will deceive at the first, if not the second glance. However, it was then discovered that the top had been cut without sufficient overhang, so a reeded moulding, which can be bought by the yard, was added.

You can see the added moulding in this photograph.

The piece could then be re-assembled. The handles that had been selected (true copies of eighteenth-century designs) were put on and here you have the result.

Here you see a good-looking Sheraton chest-of-drawers. It is quite convincing at first glance and would deceive most people. At second glance the knowledgeable would note the absence of the two small drawers at the top, the Victorian Bramah locks, and when he looked at the bottom he would see where the curved front had been cut through in the middle. If he removed a drawer and turned it upside down, he would notice the shiny heads of a few new nails and smell a rat; and his suspicions might be aroused by the absence of wear and patination at the sides of the drawers. But in nine cases out of ten the seller could get away with it.

Viewed from the back, you notice the inequalities of patination on the back boards, the absence of patination round the heads of the nails.

Value? The piece itself cost £15. The work on it cost £45 and a trade valuation put the present price at £165.

PART FIVE

The Pieces Themselves

The pieces illustrated in this section are, of course, all genuine, except where expressly and categorically stated to the contrary.

Bookcases, Breakfront-

A breakfront-bookcase is one with a protruding central section having shelves behind glazed doors above, and a cupboard below; and side wings where the lower sections may be cupboards but are more often drawers.

These have always been sought after and thus are expensive. The smaller they are the more they cost. Being in demand they are often copies or 'made up'. Many that you see are secretaire-bookcases, bureau-bookcases and chests-of-drawers to which wings have been added; still more started life as breakfront-wardrobes which have been reduced from front to back and have had the wood panels of the doors removed and the doors glazed with old glass. Often, the two-door type of wardrobe has wings added to make it a breakfront-bookcase; but it is cheaper to convert these into china-cabinets.

Be wary of a breakfront-bookcase with square or Gothic glazing as anything with this type of glazing is easy to reduce in height. Note, too, the height of the first groove to take a shelf: if this is, say, seven inches from the bottom, then the top groove should be seven inches from the top.

If the top gap is only an inch or two this will be because the piece has been cut down, *not* because that shelf was intended for butterflies or eggshells. (See also *Shelf Supports*.)

The top section of a breakfront-bookcase should always be higher than the bottom section and there should be a moulding round it where it stands on the bottom section.

The frames holding the glass in the top part should be of exactly the same width as those holding the wooden panels below. Glazing is usually all of the same pattern in the wings and in the centre section.

In the more valuable pieces, the wings are nearly always of the same height as the central part.

The bottom of the wings can consist of drawers or cupboards. The great majority with drawers had four on either side, sometimes five. Three is a suspect number.

Check the writing height when the flap is down (2′ 6″–2′ 8″).

Look for three plugged screwholes high up on the inside of the top part. The presence of these shows that the piece started life as a wardrobe and the holes are where the socket carrying the rod or rail was fixed to the side.

Bookcases, Bureau-

A bureau-bookcase is one where the upper part is a bookcase with blind or glazed doors, and the lower part a bureau – that is, a chest-of-drawers, surmounted by a writing section

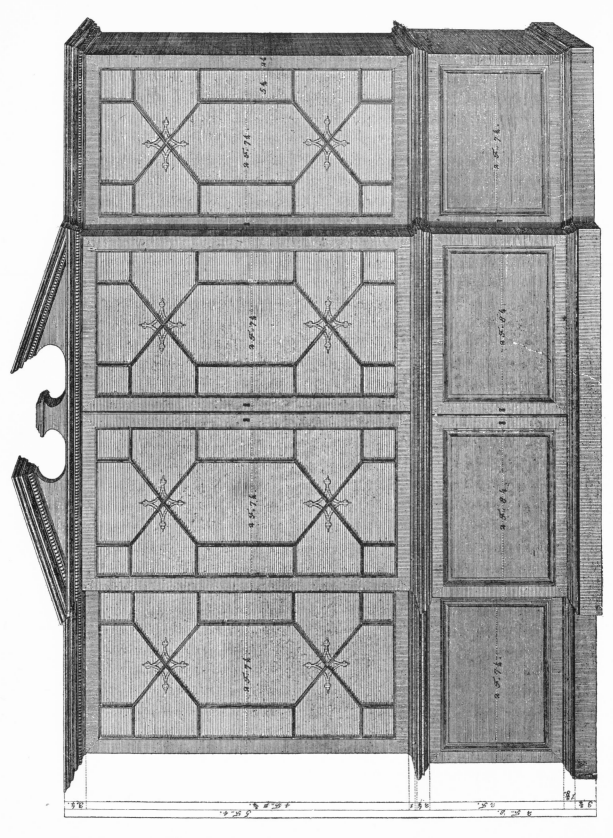

44 Library or breakfront-bookcase.

45 Bureau-bookcase.

behind a sloping front, which lets down and is supported on lopers to form the writing surface.

The criteria for judging the double-heighted piece (see p. 49) again applies here. Top and bottom parts should be of the same thickness. Where there is any inlay, ensure that the wood used, the design and so forth are the same on both parts. Watch the proportions of top and bottom. The timbers used for the sides and backs should be the same in both sections, as should the size and design of the escutcheons.

The bottom part of a bureau-bookcase should have either four long drawers, or two short drawers, side by side, with three long ones underneath. In William and Mary and early Queen Anne pieces, there was a dummy drawer hiding a well (see when the flap is down) with two short and two long drawers, or three long drawers beneath it. If there are books on the shelves, have them out. They may be hiding shelf-grooves that are too clean to be old, or some other sign of tampering.

Watch the writing heights: if more or less than 2' 6"–2' 8", the piece is suspect.

Many of the pieces you see are 'marriages' (see p. 62). Sometimes where the top part is tall, one drawer in the bottom part is done away with, making the writing height ridiculously low.

These bookcases were often originally made with blind doors – that is with wood panels. Many have had these panels removed and glass substituted. This can usually be detected (see p. 54). The number of panes in glazed doors is usually thirteen. Only Chippendale glazing entailed fifteen, eighteen or twenty-one panes.

Bookcases, Secretaire-

The secretaire-bookcase differs from the bureau-bookcase chiefly in the arrangement of the writing section, which is in fact the top drawer of the bottom part. This drawer pulls out and the front of it can be let down on curved hinges to make a flat writing surface. Underneath are either two cupboards or three drawers (not two). The drawers should run the full depth. The top sections of secretaire-bookcases are nearly always glazed.

46 Secretaire-bookcase.

47 Bureau.

The usual double-height criteria will apply (see p. 49).

The small secretaire-bookcase of 3′ 6″ width sells for about £350; those of 3′ 9″ and 4′ 5″ are too big for modern tastes and are usually reduced or made into china-cabinets (see p. 31). Many a secretaire-chest has had a top part added to it to make it into a secretaire-bookcase.

Bureaux

The smaller bureaux are the more popular (and valuable) and many of the 4′ 0″ bureaux are cut down to 2′ 6″ and similarly reduced in depth.

Others have tops added to make them bureau-bookcases. A large William and Mary bureau can be bought for £150 or so, a top made for £80 and the resulting bureau-bookcase sold for £950. A bureau has sometimes two short drawers and three long drawers, or four long drawers; or three long drawers and a top dummy drawer. If there is a dummy drawer there will be a well for keeping papers under the slide, which you find when the writing flap is down. This slide pushes back revealing the well.

Candlesticks

If you buy a pair of wood candlesticks, make sure they have circular bases. To be genuine period they should have a ring of lead countersunk into the base. This was done to prevent them falling over when a large candle was used. You may have to ease the felt off to see the lead, but it must be there. If buying a pair, examine both. One may be genuine, the other just a copy.

Many candlesticks you see today are made from the very top part of the posts of a four-poster bed and the bases are new and will not have the lead circle. Some may have the shafts filled with lead shot to make them appear weighted.

Canterbury

A Canterbury is a small stand with several open-topped partitions for holding bound volumes of music. It is said that the earliest was made in 1806 for the Archbishop of Canterbury.

The earliest Canterburies have square

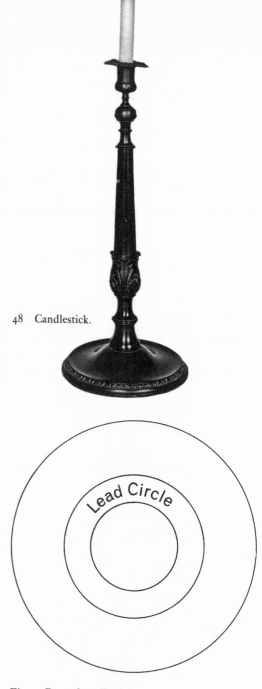

48   Candlestick.

Lead Circle

Fig 5   Base of candlestick.

tapered legs and two or three divisions, and a drawer in the base.

Round tapered legs were not made until 1810.

Many you see today were made from the base of a whatnot, but far more are of recent manufacture.

gallery was for the plates; the box for the cutlery.

The horseshoe-shaped rail on top of the spindles should be made like three-ply: that is, three strips glued to each other for strength.

In the many copies made today this small but important detail is overlooked.

49 Canterbury.

50 Plate and cutlery carrier.

Card-Tables see Tables

Carriers (for Cutlery and Plates)

These were used for taking cutlery and plates about a room. The section with the spindle

The Victorians also made many copies, giving them heavy and ugly turned legs. Today the careful restorer will turn the legs smaller, making them more graceful, but in doing this he will inevitably destroy the patination and open the grain, which will tell you what has been done.

Chairs

Chairs, perhaps, are the most sought-after antiques and often relatively very expensive. Fortunately it is easy to tell whether they are genuine or not. When buying a chair or a set of chairs turn them upside down and make sure that the seat rails are all the same and have the same depth of patination. There should be equal patination on the underside of both arms of an armchair. Also remember that armchairs are always wider across the front than single chairs.

All the best cabinet-makers had workshops in London and all London-made chairs had the arms put on from the side of the back leg. (Country-made chairs may be period as far as date is concerned, but they do not measure up in quality.)

Remember, too, that the top rail of a period chair must never overhang the sides, but must be contained within the two back legs. If the chair you look at has a different seat rail or arm, or patination, you will know that it started life as a settee. Writing chairs or desk chairs are often made from a settee. If the 'converter' makes one chair from the settee, it will be almost undetectable, but if, as usual, he is greedy and makes two, each will have to have a complete new side and that you will detect.

Always remove hessian, which can hide such faults as one seat rail being different from the other, or even all the seat rails being new. Don't accept it, if you are told they were replaced because of worm.

Where there is carving, make sure that this is not flat, as is all carving added to a chair after it has been made.

Watch the cross stretcher rails. If these are strangely low (only an inch or so off the ground), you will know that the legs have been cut.

Hepplewhite was famous for the shield shape of his chairs, but he never made a shield that ended in a sharp point. His shield points are all blunt.

The seat of the best quality Windsor chair will usually be of elm and the legs of yew. The best have four cabriole legs, but every good one will have two cabriole legs in front. Any with round, turned legs are Victorian or later.

Windsor chairs were made in many country districts from about 1720, but the best came from Windsor, hence the name.

A chair which has a stuff-over seat or back and is shaped, bow-fronted or serpentine-fronted, will fetch a bigger price than a straight-fronted one. Make sure the shaping is done with the wood and not just the upholstery, as many are stuffed out with cotton wool to give them a shape.

If buying a wing-chair or similar upholstered chair, where just four legs are seen, you will find the frame is made of birch or beech. (As this is covered with the upholstery, there is no need to use an elegant timber for it.) The four legs can be walnut or mahogany and the rest of the back legs from just above the seat rail will be spliced to these; so if you run your hand down over the upholstery of the back legs, you should be able to feel where it is spliced, because the soft wood will have dried out and shrunk away from the walnut or mahogany.

MEASUREMENTS:

Width of seat of simple chair 1′ 8″ to 1′ 10″
Width of seat of arm chair   1′ 10½″ to 2′ 2″
Height of *all* chair seat
furniture from floor to
top of seat   1′ 6″

Chair arms

The arms of a chair were always fixed to the sides of the back supports, not to the front.

51   Chair with arms fixed correctly.

Both the arms and arm uprights were fixed. The uprights were attached to the seat rails by two screws and the arms were fixed to the side of the back legs with one screw. In doing this, the chair makers first drilled the holes, then countersunk the screws at least half an inch below the surface; they then plugged the holes with circular pieces (dowels) of the *same* timber as that with which the chair was made. Thus, you do not see the screws and if the armchair is genuine you should not today see the circular dowels, as they will have blended with the rest of the chair. If you *do* see these dowels, then either the arms have been added or it is a chair that has been made in or since the Victorian period.

A 'restorer' may add arms correctly (i.e. from the back) to make an ordinary armchair but even then the width of the seat will give him away, as the seat of an armchair is 2″ to $2\frac{1}{2}$″ wider than that of the single chair. If he pads out the front and corners of the chair, to which arms are added to give it some extra width (1″ to $1\frac{1}{2}$″ on either side) that will help to make it look genuine, but this will not be enough to be convincing. The padding will be soft. If the width is genuine, you should be able to feel the wood of the frame underneath the padding.

Some people consider that the reading chair is just a polite term for the old cock-fighting chair, which has been adapted because cock-fighting became illegal. Whichever they are, when you used them you sat with your back to the front and had your arms on the rests.

The drawer was used for keeping the cock's spurs, if they were cock-fighting chairs, and the book support for betting slips. These chairs are often faked, mostly from corner chairs, so look for old castors (green, mouldy colour), old candle-holders and brass studs and, of course, patination.

Chandeliers (brass)

The branches of a genuine old chandelier must be solid, so take a pencil and tap them to

52   Bachelor chest.

see how they ring. If they ring hollow, the chandelier is either modern or has been interfered with.

Many have come from churches.

As a general rule, the longer the sweep of the branches, the earlier the chandelier. Those with long sweeps will be English. The Dutch chandeliers have shorter branches. Don't buy any with holes drilled to take wires for electric lights; if you want them wired run the wire along the outside of the branches.

Chests, Bachelor

The bachelor chests, made of walnut or mahogany, were almost always relatively shallow from back to front, usually 10″, and they were seldom more than 2′ 9″ wide. They had either two small drawers and three long drawers, or four long drawers. On either side of the top drawer were lopers to carry the flat top when unfolded. Many chests – of drawers and bureaux are made into bachelor chests (see p. 30). These will have had to be reduced, particularly from back to front, and as a result, the drawers will most likely be front-heavy (with a tendency to fall forward when you pull them far out). This reduction often puts the feet out of proportion to the new size of the chest, so watch that.

Watch, too, the hinges on the top flap which must be of the scissors (rule joint) type, and work from the outside edge into which they will be countersunk.

Make sure the number of drawers is correct. Card-table tops and flaps of bureaux are often used to fake the tops.

Chest-of-drawers

A chest-of-drawers had either two small and three long, or four long drawers.

Many that you see have three short drawers

at the top and, almost invariably, these will have been made from the top of a tallboy and so are not a genuine chest-of-drawers. They will have new feet and a new top board. Although the top board will have been made of old timber such as a leaf of a dining table, the back edge, where the timber has been cut, will have no patination, so always look at the back edges to be sure that there is patination where it should be and enough of it for the presumed age of the piece.

53a

Here is a chest-of-drawers (53a) sold honestly and for a sensible price as a made-up piece. Looking at it, I would say it had been made from a tallboy, using even the cornice round the top. The two small drawers and the

53b A perfect 4-drawer chest-of-drawers.

three long ones are of a type often found on the top of a tallboy, the feet and the fourth long drawer from the bottom, could also come from the same tallboy. The sides appear to have been re-veneered to hide an ugly join.

Other evidence of a chest having been made from a tallboy is (a) blind fret on the angles and below the top board; (b) columns at the corners, and (d) large overhang of the top, sometimes disguised by the insertion of a baize-topped slide. Often the feet that served the tallboy are used for the chest, but these are too large and cumbersome for a chest of drawers and look out of proportion.

Chiffonier

The chiffonier is a small cupboard. Many have one or two open shelves and an enclosed cupboard beneath. Originally made in mahogany or satinwood, the very late ones were often made of rosewood, sometimes with ornate brass embellishments. They are very popular and are now manufactured in large numbers. The doors of a chiffonier often had grille fronts (see *Grille*).

Many you see today started life as a boot cupboard. Open the doors and you will see where the original grooves have been filled in.

These grooves were slanted downwards from the front to the back, so that the shelves slanted in the proper way for shoes.

54 A period chiffonier.

China-cabinets

The first were made by Dutch cabinet-makers about 1600. The genuine ones are essentially two-height pieces, with shelves behind glazed doors on top and a cupboard below.

Many are made out of wardrobes and these give themselves away by having sides all in one piece. Others are made from the larger and less popular secretaire-bookcases of 3′ 9″ to 4′ 0″ wide with cupboards below (see p. 31), and here the removal of the secretaire part makes the piece low-waisted and the proportions wrong. Others are marriages of different tops and bottoms, usually revealed by differences in escutcheons, in width of the stiles of the door frames, or in timber.

China-cabinets made from wardrobes will inevitably have new glazing, which is easily detectable (see p. 54).

Watch the hinges, escutcheons and timbers. If the piece seems low-waisted, open the cupboard and look inside: if you can see holes in the top that have been plugged, or the timber of the top is different to that of the sides and bottom, the piece will probably have started life as a wardrobe or secretaire-bookcase.

Commode

This name is given both to a kind of cupboard and to a chest on tall legs; the commode-chest will have either two long drawers, or three long drawers, or two small drawers and two long drawers. (The ordinary chest-of-drawers has either two small drawers and three long drawers, or four long drawers.)

Many 'commodes' on the market today are the bottom parts of tallboys to which a top and four bracket feet have been added. These tops are often made from the leaf of a dining table, so have a look at the back edge to make sure there is patination. The commode chest goes back to 1708 in Paris and 1760 in England. It always has tall legs.

Many of the cupboard type are made from a side table, which will have had four square tapered legs, the taper being always on the inside of the leg. No cabinet-maker ever tried to screw a door on to a tapering leg, but the faker will. Others are made from one half-round end of a leg dining table; here too the doors hang wrongly. More important yet, the height of a dining table is 2′ 4″, that of most commodes is 3′ 0″ which means that the fake's legs have had to be made longer. This is done by adding six or seven inches and bandaging the join (see p. 42). Commodes are also made from the top half of a gentleman's wardrobe, to which new feet and a new top board have been added. When you open the doors of an ex-wardrobe commode, you may see graze marks made by the trays when

55 China cabinet.

56 A period commode.

the wardrobe was serving its original purpose (see p. 55).

Cupboards, Bedside

As a general rule you can say that Chippendale bedside-cupboards were made singly and Sheraton ones in pairs, to stand one on either side of the bed. In the latter, one door will open to the left, the other to the right. A pair will be worth ten times the value of a single piece, so often two opening the same way are bought, the door on one altered to open the other way and there you have a pair. These cupboards were made to hold a chamber-pot

(of pewter): if you buy one with the pot still there, it will put the value up £30.

The bedside-cupboard must have a rail or moulding round the sides. If the top is flush it will not be period.

The base inside, on which the chamber-pot stood, was never a solid piece of wood, but made of three or four slats. This was to let air circulate. Nine out of every ten on the market today were made in Victorian times and are not slatted.

Cupboards, Corner-

The corner-cupboard is essentially a double-

57 Designs for pot-cupboards by Hepplewhite.

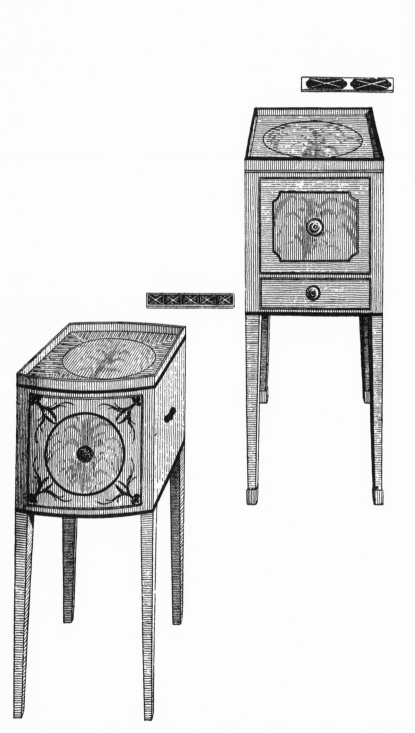

heighted piece, thus the side timbers and top and bottom should be from the same piece of wood, as should the timbers in the back boards. In the last ten years I myself have seen only three genuine double-heighted corner-cupboards; the rest were either marriages of hanging corner-cupboards, for which bottom parts had been made, or were completely new.

Pairs of corner-cupboards were *never* made; the 'pairs' one sometimes sees were fitments built into a house, not free-standing pieces; or else they were made from a large period one, which had two doors, top and bottom and was cut in half from top to bottom making a pair.

Sometimes a corner-cupboard was made open and has had doors added.

The corner-cupboard is one of the few pieces of eighteenth-century furniture in which you can see the hinges when looking at the front of it. All other doors are hinged on the face of the side timbers, so that only the knuckle of the hinge can be seen and then only from the side, or else pin hinges are used.

Desks

Pedestal- and kneehole-desks had three short drawers across the top and three short drawers in each pedestal. The three drawers in the top need not necessarily be of the same width, but the two end ones must be of the same width as the drawers beneath them in the pedestals or sides.

Some desks were made with solid tops and have had leather added later. If a desk started life with a leather top, it had its edges cross-banded. Often the addition of leather to a solid desk has been done 'on the cheap' by planing out the top to a depth of $\frac{1}{8}''$, but leaving $1''$ of timber round the outer edge

58 Corner cupboard.

to simulate crossbanding. Where this has been done the grain of the 'crossbanding' will run the same way top, bottom and at the sides, instead of running differently at the sides.

Desks, Kneehole-

The kneehole-desk is like a pedestal-desk with a recessed cupboard in the space between the two pedestals, only it is made from one piece. These desks were first made about 1714, in walnut, and had three drawers across the top with three more down each side.

Genuine ones are very rare. As they can be used as dressing-tables or writing-tables they are in great demand. Most of those you see are reproductions or fakes. Most faked kneehole-desks have been made from a chest-of-drawers, which can easily be turned into a kneehole-desk, though if it has a brushing slide below the top board, as many have, this is a give-away, for no one ever made a desk with a brushing slide. Another way to tell a conversion is to take a small drawer from each side and look at their sides. If the piece was originally a chest-of-drawers and the drawers have been reduced to make room for a cupboard, each will have a new side (nearest

59 Kneehole-desk.

the cupboard). The dovetails will be different and even though old timber has been used, if the drawers have oak sides, as they should, it will be very unlikely that the new oak will match the old in colour and grain, or that there will be the same amount of patination on either side.

Many kneehole-desks have only one drawer across the top instead of three, but still only three in each pedestal (see below).

Sometimes you will notice that the grain of the timber carries across the gap of the kneehole from one small drawer to the other showing that these were once long drawers and the 'desk' originally a chest-of-drawers.

Desks, Pedestal-

Genuine desks are made in three pieces: a top and two pedestals. They should be made of mahogany and have oak-sided drawers. On all desks made up to 1780, the timber of the bottom of each drawer will run from front to back and the drawer will have no corner mouldings inside.

A single-sided pedestal-desk will have three drawers in the top and three drawers in each pedestal and the back will be nicely finished.

The double-sided, partner's desk will have, on one side, three drawers in the top and three drawers in each pedestal and, on

60 Pedestal-desk.

the other, just three drawers in the top; the pedestal being cupboards with doors.

The timber of the sides of the top must run the same way (vertically) as the timber of the pedestals.

There are usually three drawers in each pedestal.

If the top is flush with the sides, this is *wrong*. There should be a moulding overhang.

The corners should be square.

The three drawers across the top are usually all of the same width; but you do find desks where the side drawers are narrower than the centre drawer.

The drawers in the pedestals should be the same size as those above them in the top.

Dumb-Waiter

The dumb-waiter made its appearance about 1750.

It is made of solid mahogany and has three dish top trays.

There are plenty of 'naughty' ones with only two trays.

The gallery can be spindle or fretted. Where fretted, it should be of three-ply (see *Fret*).

(Very often the top tray and tripod are married and sold as a genuine tripod table. You cannot do this with the other trays as they have holes in them.)

Knife-Boxes

Knife-boxes were always made either in pairs or in sets of three. They either have serpentine-shaped fronts and sloping lids, or are in the shape of an urn. When lifted, the lid of the urn stays up, held by a wooden spring clip, fixed to a shaft attached to the lid, which will not go down again until the spring is compressed with the fingers.

61 Dumb-waiter.

A cockleshell inlaid in the lid is a sign that the piece is either Victorian, or was inlaid in Victorian times.

Nearly all knife-boxes have an inlaid star inside their lids.

If you buy a pair with the original cutlery inside it will be a real find.

62a   Urn-shaped knife boxes.

62b   Knife-boxes with serpentine-shaped fronts.

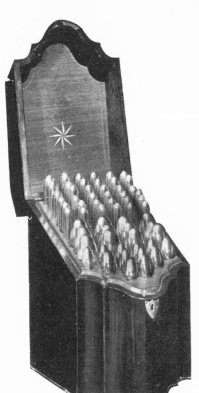
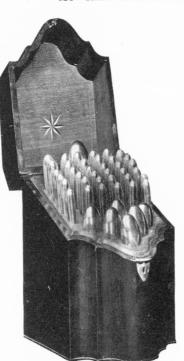
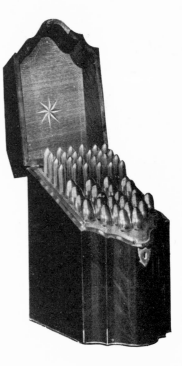

62c & 62d Eighteenth-century designs for knife-boxes or cases. The vase-shaped ones are rarer and therefore more valuable.

Lacquer

Pieces used to be sent to China for lacquering and every piece decorated in this way was signed with (usually) two Chinese characters on the underneath of the seat rail, or, if it had drawers, the front and sides were lacquered all over, but a space for the lacqueror's initials was left on the back.

Good lacquering can be done outside China today, the characters often being painted on by some obliging Chinese. Old lacquer is now crinkled, rather like crackle glaze. The whole piece was lacquered, legs included. If any part is painted, that will be restoration or disguise. (For illustration see *Screen*). Japanese lacquer can only be identified by the scene and/or lack of signature. It is not nearly so valuable.

Mirrors

The peoples of antiquity mirrored themselves in polished metal. The silvered looking-glass was not invented until the early Renaissance and was very costly. It was mainly available in small pieces which were given important frames to exaggerate their size and emphasize the value.

Mirror plate could not be made in large sizes in England until late in the eighteenth century, which is why William and Mary, Queen Anne and many Chippendale mirrors were made in two or three pieces.

Mirror glass was expensive. Most of it came from Italy and was sold at auction by Christie's. In 1618 imports were prohibited by Act of Parliament until 1624, and the same thing happened in 1635 and 1664. In 1674 the Duke of Buckingham opened the Vauxhall glass works where Venetian craftsmen worked.

The early mirrors were blown. The hot molten glass was blown into a long cylinder, which was laid on a metal tray and slit along its length with shears. It was then put back in the furnace, where the heat made the slit open, and the halves fell away until both flaps were lying flat on the tray. A man could only blow the molten glass to about 3′ 4″ in length: thus a mirror of any great length, or breadth, had to be made in several pieces. The glass was thinnest at the edge farthest from the blower's mouth, and this thin end was always put to the top of the frame. In all but the smaller mirrors, therefore, the top corners of the frame were always made rounded on the inside, so as to hide the thin piece of mirror at the top. There are experts who maintain that the inside top corners of eighteenth-century mirrors could be square; but the more I see of old mirror glass of the period and realize the difficulty of getting a neat square edge on it, the more convinced I am that the top corners of most eighteenth-century mirrors were rounded.

All mirrors, whether gilded, mahogany or walnut, have a pine frame underneath. This is because pine was cheap, soft and easy to carve, and light in weight. All frames should be made of wood (remember a pin sticks in wood but *not* in plaster). The backs of mirrors will show patination just as other pieces of furniture.

Frames are made of four pieces of wood (two sides, a top and a bottom).

The mirror plate of all old mirrors is silvered and the bevel is just a thin wavy line and difficult to see today. The thinner the mirror plate, the older it is likely to be. The easiest way to tell the thickness of mirror plate without removing it from the frame is to take a silver coin and put the milled edge against the glass and hold it there slightly tilted; the distance between the actual coin and the reflection will be the thickness of the glass.

(If you have to replace the mirror or plate

in an old mirror, blacken the four freshly cut edges of the plate before putting it in the mirror frame, then when you look in the mirror you will not see the edges.)

When it got broken or became blackened, the old glass was replaced, usually from the front as that was easiest. It made the job simpler if the top corners of the frame were squared off, and you can sometimes see where this has been done. Square top corners in a wall mirror are thus (to me) suspect. If they are not the result of a later alteration, they may mean that the mirror was originally a picture frame.

When a tall mirror was made it was in several pieces, the joins between the pieces were hidden by an astragal bar. Often when new glass has been put in, this has been in one piece and the bars have been removed to allow this. You will probably be able to see the marks where the bars used to fit into the sides.

The four 'ears' of a mirror must be the same.

Walnut mirrors will be walnut veneer on a pine frame. The tops of almost all walnut and mahogany mirrors are warped. This is because the heat of the room over the years warps the soft pine frame. The gilt bird on top of many such mirrors is usually carved out of pine and you will often see cracks in its belly. On a convex mirror the bird should look to the left. You will occasionally see a dragon or griffin instead of a bird (eagle): these are often later additions.

Many restorers have thought a bird perched on top would add to the value of the piece and have given it one, spoiling the proportions in doing so. Original birds are usually attached by two screws, if on a convex mirror, or carved in the top section of other mirrors.

The best convex mirrors have a carved eagle on top and carved leaves on the bottom.

It is most important that there is an inner black circle glued to the mirror. This was always present in old convex mirrors made before 1850, and consists of four to five reeds.

Convex mirrors with frames like tyres are very late, probably Victorian.

Mirrors, toilet

Here, as with other mirrors, the frames of those that are genuinely old and period have rounded top corners to hide the edge of the glass.

The Sheraton ones are of oval or shield shape on a bow-fronted or serpentine base, with three drawers. The base will be mahogany as will the upright, but the frame will be of pine faced with mahogany (except at the back). The oval is made of three hoops of pine one inside the other (the front and sides veneered with mahogany); thus from the back you should see the three loops of the frame. It was made this way for strength.

Here is a genuine example (though I think the stretcher might be a later addition) with the correct oval mirror.

Needlework

If you are told that the chair, stool etc. you are considering has original needlework, have two or three of the tacks holding it removed and inspect underneath. If there are *no* other tack holes, the needlework will most probably be original; but if there are other tack holes, it means that some other upholstery was there before.

The needlework will, indeed, be old; but in all probability off a firescreen and may have been added quite recently. Added needlework like this often has to have extra pieces of canvas or other material tacked on, especially at the sides. Obviously, original

63 Toilet table.

needlework would have been made on a piece of canvas of the right size.

Plate-Buckets

As kitchens were often a long way from the dining room, plates were heated and carried to the dining room in buckets, nearly all of which have a slot or part of the side open so that you could get at the plates easily. The early ones have open fret sides.

Plate-buckets were often made in pairs.

64   George III plate-bucket (1795).

They are now popular for use in flower arrangements and so are manufactured. Look for patination on free edges. There should be plenty. Check the colour of the brass.

Screens, Fold

There are two criteria for these screens: that there is an even number of folds and that the picture is complete and continuous on all folds, whether made of wood or leather, painted or lacquered (See p. 130).

Make sure the ends of a screen are there as these will show that the screen is complete. Otherwise there will be hinge marks.

Lacquered screens were made in England and sent to China to be lacquered.

Screens, Pole

The purpose of the pole-screen was to keep the heat of the fire off a lady's face when she was sitting by the fireside. Whether women

65   Pole-screen.

are no longer so careful of their complexions or fires are not so hot, such screens have long been out of fashion. Now, most are converted into tripod-tables but as the height of a pole-screen, designed to protect the face of a seated person, is considerably lower than that of such a table, some eight inches have to be added. The join can usually be detected, if only because the grain of the wood is different.

Shelves, fretted

You see very few genuine fretted shelves.

The two chief criteria are (a) that the pattern of each shelf is different (two were never made the same) and (b) that the fretted sides were made of three pieces of wood glued together for strength and not from a solid piece.

These shelves were first made in 1750 and are always of mahogany.

Look for tool marks. If these are visible, the shelves are not two hundred years old, for in two centuries the marks of saw and chisel will have become smoothed away (see *Fret*).

Sideboards

No genuine eighteenth-century sideboard has just four legs. They all had six.

All sideboards made in our period had tops made from one piece of timber. These Georgian tops often warped, so the Victorians took to making theirs in two or three pieces with the result that the warping of one or more split the veneer. If you see a sideboard with a repair right along the top you can be sure that it was made after 1860.

The best genuine period sideboard had a serpentine or bow front, six legs and was crossbanded on top. Its drawers would have

oak sides and cock-beading; it had two deep cellarette drawers and one centre drawer.

The legs were all made of one piece of timber from the floor to underneath the top. (Inlaid lines or beading may hide a join, and a join *must* be 'naughty'.)

Sideboards are easy to reduce in length but they must also be reduced from back to front to keep them in proportion (see p. 27) so always feel along the underside of the overlap at the side for a join (where the piece was cut out to reduce the depth of the top), and look underneath in case the converter glued a thin piece of veneer over the join to hide it. You should also turn the piece over on its top, remove the drawers and if there is a join in the top (showing that it has been reduced or is Victorian), you will see it.

All good sideboards have a top that slightly overhangs at the front, sides and back.

(For illustration see p. 132.)

Sometimes a sideboard has a cupboard at one end. This was for a chamber-pot. (I wonder if there were two-pot men, as well as two-bottle ones?)

Turned legs can be late Sheraton (1795), but are mostly Victorian.

A 'Scotch' sideboard is one which has a platform on top (Sheraton period).

Stools

Many stools are made out of chairs, so examine the underside of the seat rails and if one (or more) has a Roman numeral scratched or carved on it, it will tell you that the stool was made from one or more chairs of a set.

Genuine period stools are very rare, and transformation into a stool raises the value of a chair ten or twenty times. So beware especially of hessian under the seat; this was never used before 1840 and today hides sins.

Rounded corners are another sign of the

66 Lacquered fold screen.

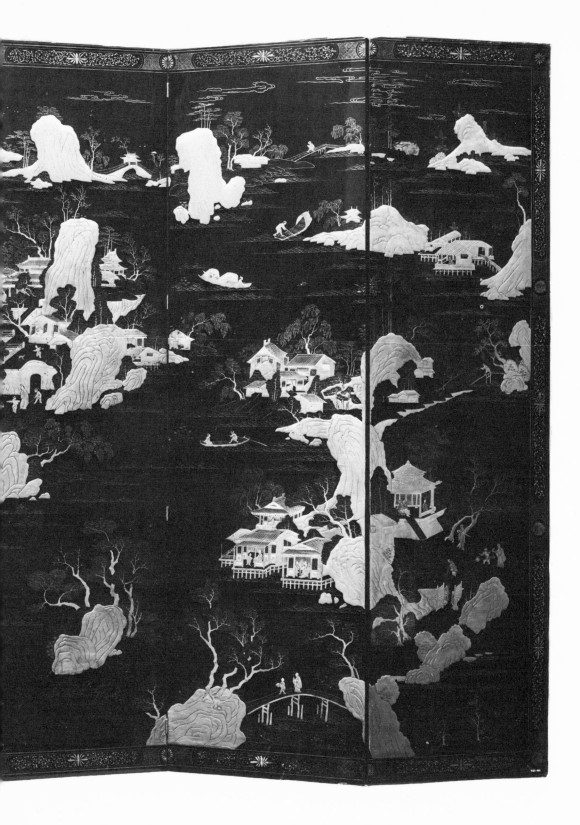

'stool' having been a chair originally.

As stools are frequently handled, there ought to be extra thick patination on the places where you would pick it up.

In one case a pair of chairs was made into one stool, and had numbers on each of the front and back seat rails. The chairs were genuine George I or II with backs in one piece of veneer (if they had been Queen Anne the veneer would have been quartered) and this made them worth only £80. The stool that was made out of them fetched £725, so the conversion was well worth it. The stool had 'original' needlework.

67   Sideboard.

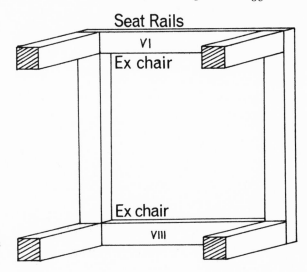

Seat Rails

VI

Ex chair

Ex chair

VIII

68 Diagram showing underside of rails on a stool. The two roman numerals indicate that the stool has been made from two chairs.

Tables in general

Victorian games-, leg, writing-, Pembroke and work-tables were often made with pedestal supports; today the restorer removes the pedestal, plugs the four or six holes where the pedestal was screwed on and puts on four square tapered legs which enables him to say the table was sixty years, or more, earlier in date. He may even paint the whole underside of the table with a pink stain: if you see that, beware!

A good restorer can take ugly circular (Victorian) legs, turn them to half their width and then box them in with four pieces of thick veneer. When finished the legs are tapered on the inside and that makes the table eighteenth-century (see *Legs*). To hide what has been done there will usually be a metal dome of silence on the bottom of the leg, or the bottom may be veneered; the best restorers will put on box castors, but the colour and finish of the legs will still be different to that of the rest of the table and give the game away.

Table Pedestals

Pedestals supporting a dining or other table ought to have four legs, not three. The more rings on a pedestal, the later it will be.

If a table top has a reeded edge, the legs should also be reeded. If the legs had ugly knees which have been removed, the easiest way to tell is by running the palm of your hand slowly up along the legs from the castor to the column. If knees have been removed, the surface at the top of the legs will feel smoother than that near the castors, while the edges of the reeding will be sharper.

Table, Architect's

The so-called architect's table has a top that rises, the height being adjusted by a ratchet and easel. There is a large flap which can be fixed horizontally as a table and, usually, the whole front will pull out with the two front legs, which are made to fit flush with the centre legs so that they look like one.

An architect's table is often turned into a writing-table by fastening down the top and lining it with leather; the front and front legs may be fastened to the sides and part of the front used to make one or two drawers, which means that the sides, bottoms and backs of the drawers will be new and that there will be no wear or patination on the sides: or, if the legs were shaped the table will probably be left to pull out, though it will still be given drawers (with new bottoms, sides and backs) and a new top. I have known cases where this made it 'Sheraton'.

69 Architect's table.

Tables, Book-

Book-tables were not thought of until very
late in our period. A patent for the circular
revolving type shown here was taken out in
1808. Another kind, like a sofa-table with
usually three shelves, was probably first
made about 1820. This type had shelves on
either side of a centrepiece.

In genuine book-tables, many of the books
are dummies, for neither construction would
withstand the weight of a full load of real
books.

Tables, Breakfast

Although the earliest type of breakfast-table,
of about 1720-30, had four legs the ones
usually sold today have oval (the best) or
rectangular tops on a slender shaft and a
splay of four legs with box castors. The top
tilts up for the table to be put out of the way.
The top should preferably be made from one
piece of timber, but such are rare. The top
will be cross-banded and this crossbanding
will be separated from the main timber of the
top by a line or lines of inlay. If this inlay is
countersunk or level with the top, to my mind
the table will be 'naughty'. If genuine, you
should feel the dividing line as you run your
fingers across the main timber and cross-
banding because shrinkage of the main timber
will have forced the inlay up. Release the
brass catch and tilt the table up and you
should see up to six inches of thick patination
all round the underside. If there is no
patination it means either that the top is new
or that it has been reshaped, probably from
an oblong top. If you see plugged holes
underneath, you will know that the top has
been made from something else.

Also run your hand down the four legs, for
if the pedestal was made in Victorian times, it
probably had ugly knees which may have

70 Book-table.

been removed and four or five reeded lines
engraved on each leg instead. If the edges feel
sharp or new this will probably be the reason,
for no table that has been in use for two
hundred years or so, with people's feet
kicking the legs, will have sharp edges now.

Any table of this type with an apron round
the top is Victorian. So is a platform-base.
Look for screwholes on the underside of oval
tables. If there are any, it means that it must
have had an apron at one time.

71 Breakfast-table.

There was another type of breakfast-table with two flaps at either end (like a Pembroke table) and a wire cage underneath the top, into which the staff placed the food if anyone was late, in order, presumably, to prevent the cat or dog stealing it. An example of this type of table is illustrated here.

72 Card-table.

Tables, Card-

Card-tables get a lot of handling, in opening and shutting them and in moving them about, so there should always be considerable patination underneath. Look at both edges of the top, for they must be the same colour.

If buying a pair, turn them both upside down: they should look alike underneath. A single Sheraton card-table can be bought for £30, but a pair costs £500 or so: thus there are many 'pairs', one of which is old and genuine, the other reproduction or converted Victorian.

The earliest period card-tables have a concertina action, in which both back legs and back frame open together to support the fold-over top; if two back legs open it is a better piece than if just one opens.

If the top swings on a pedestal, it is Victorian.

Card-tables are oblong, square or circular (when opened out), and serpentine.

73 Drum-table.

74   Games-table.

Tables, Dressing-

The criterion of a period dressing-table is that it should open in one way or another to bring a mirror into use (see p. 126).

Tables, Drum

The drum table was used for writing. It should have four drawers and four dummy drawers, and it should be on a nice, graceful pedestal, preferably with four reeded legs ending in box castors.

There are genuine Sheraton drum tables, but infinitely more Victorian ones, which are now bought and 'converted'. If the drawers go to a point at the back, the piece is wrong. Drum table drawers were always of the normal shape.

Some drum tables have a deep frieze with deep drawers. These are not considered very saleable, but it is an easy matter to unscrew the top board, reduce the height of the drawers and there you have a very saleable table.

Tables, Games-

Not being much in demand, games-tables are not faked. They were made by all the big makers well into Victorian times.

Chippendale and Sheraton made theirs mostly of mahogany.

The Victorians loved walnut and dark heavy markings and the crab type of leg. The crab leg was very strong and often used in cheval mirrors where there was considerable weight to be supported.

Tables, Hunting-

These were tables used for serving drinks before or after a hunt, usually outdoors. The earliest were made in 1820. They had ugly circular legs which could be unscrewed so that the tables could be taken some distance away or even put in a brake. They were always semi-circular with a loose section which, when not in use, could be used as a side table. They were always made of mahogany. I have seen a fake made in satinwood, which fact alone gave it away.

Hunting-tables were never made with tripod shafts.

Tables, Nest-of-

The first nest-of-tables was made in about 1806. The old nests were always made of four or five tables, Sheraton appearing to have been the first to nest only three. They are at least 2′ 6″ in height. The early ones were made of mahogany. The great majority of the rosewood nests were made between 1800 and 1902. Overleaf is an example of a genuine one.

75 Hunting-table.

76 Nest-of-tables.

Tables, Pedestal-Dining

Width at least 4′0″ (up to 6′0″); height 2′4″. A pedestal-dining table can have either two pedestals and one leaf, *or* three pedestals and two leaves *or* four pedestals and three leaves *or* five pedestals and four leaves.

It should be four feet across at least. Some are as much as six feet. The average two-pedestal table is about 4′6″ wide and 9′0″ long with the leaf. The height is 28″.

The genuine period dining table was always perfectly plain, so avoid one with any inlay.

Look for at least six inches of patination on the underside and feel that there are no sharp edges on the legs.

No bearers should be seen near the edge of the top; on all old tables they were chamfered off so that they are not visible beneath the table top.

Four legs on each pedestal are better than three.

If the edge of the top is plain, the legs will

77a Pedestal-table.

be plain; if it is reeded, the legs must be reeded too. Run your fingers up the reeding on the legs; if the edges of the reeding become perceptibly smoother and sharper towards the top, it may mean that the pedestal is Victorian and started life with ugly knees, which have been removed and the legs freshly reeded at these points.

There is a variant of the dining table called the Cumberland dining table. This consists of a table with two pedestal ends and curved central piece. Today these are mostly split up, a leaf being added to the two ends to make them a separate 'period' table and the centre part being sold as a separate table.

77b Here is another genuine period pedestal-table, but this is later, as is shown by the number of rings on the shaft and the 'heaviness' about the legs.

78 Pembroke table.

Tables, Pembroke

The Pembroke table is a table with a narrow centre part and two flaps that can be supported on fly rails. Those with oval or serpentine-shaped tops are much more valuable than those with square tops, which have obvious practical disadvantages. On tables with shaped tops, the ends where the drawer is should be bow-fronted. Each flap of a good Pembroke table should be supported by two fly rails, not one. Remember no matter how small a table is, each flap has at least three hinges.

No Pembroke table is genuine eighteenth-century, if the insides of the legs do not taper, or if the tops of the legs are not the same width as the side frames of the drawer.

79 Rent-table.

Tables, Rent-

These are like drum tables, only the base is a cupboard, not a pedestal. They were made for use on large estates where many tenants came to pay rent. They have a circular or polygonal lid which moves when released by a catch in the space of one of the drawers (which had first to be taken out), allowing the money to drop into a lead-lined cupboard below. Genuine ones are very rare. Some which pretend to be rent-tables have been converted from drum tables and have had a circle of gold leaf put in the centre of the new leather liner to make it look as though it covers a hole. Ask to be shown the catch that works the centre piece.

The plinth round the base of rent-tables should be of approximately the same depth as the drawers. The deeper the plinth, the later the piece is likely to be. Dealers sometimes play safe by having the plinth reduced, but as a result the whole pedestal looks out of proportion. A rent-table top can be put on a pedestal and sold as a drum table.

Tables, Side

The genuine 4′ 0″ semi-circular side table is much sought after to convert into the more profitable commode by building around the legs. Thus most of the pairs of side tables you see were the two ends of a leg dining-table. The legs, of course, have had to be heightened by 3″ (the join being hidden by a bandage, see p. 42). If the back edge is fresh, or has three or four plugged holes or round marks, where pegs to carry the leaf have been sawn flush, you will know that its origins were not as represented.

Side tables that are 5′ 0″, 6′ 0″ or 7′ 0″ long are very deep from front to back, so most are reduced in size. Be extra careful if one has a drawer. When such large side tables were made, they did not have a drawer, so any drawer will have been added, using part of the frieze as the drawer front. The rest of the drawer will be new.

81 Silver-table.

Tables, Silver-

Silver-tables were invented by Chippendale. Nearly all have an open fretted gallery. Like all fretwork (see p. 54), the gallery should be made from three-layer laminated wood. If the gallery is cut from solid wood it is certainly not period.

82 Sofa-table.

Tables, Sofa-

Genuine sofa-tables are very rare. Many that you see, if not entirely new, are based on old cheval mirror supports. Some have been converted out of a dough trough; almost anything is used.

If the stretcher-rail is turned, and has a square block in the centre, it will show that this was once one of the uprights of a mirror. The thumbscrew that held the mirror at the selected angle went into the square part. The hole for it will now be plugged and veneered or disguised with a patera.

Some old sofa-tables have deep drawers which are considered undesirable, but it is very easy to unscrew the top and reduce the height of the drawers. Once the top is screwed back you cannot detect what has been done, and the sofa-table is much more 'desirable' and expensive.

Again, remember two fly-rails support the flaps and three hinges hold the flaps.

83　Tripod-table.

84   Torchère.

Tables, Tripod

Genuine period tripod tables are also rare. Most that you see are a marriage of a tray and an old tripod from a fire-screen or torchère, or even part of the front post of a four-poster bed.

There are three things to look for:

(1) in genuine period tripod tables you never get both parts carved: either the top is carved and the tripod perfectly plain, or the tripod is carved and the top plain, dish-top or pie-crust edge;

(2) if the top is eighteenth-century and circular, whether plain, pie-crust or a dish-top, the timbers will have shrunk by now and if you measure from north to south and from east to west, you will find a difference of half an inch or so. An extra piece can be put into a top to fake this difference. So if you see the top is made of three pieces, you will know this has been done;

(3) the shaft of the tripod must be in one piece of timber, running from between the three legs to the table top.

Always pick a tripod table up and spin it slowly in your hands and note the grain of the shaft: it should be all the same and run the length of the shaft. The tripod of a fire-screen is always lower than that needed for a table so it has to be built up.

Torchères

The best, or at least the safest torchères to buy, are those with an open stand like this one. These are expensive to fake, and not worth while when there are still pole-screens to be had from which to make them. These are often given away by the fact that the top and bottom nulling often runs different ways and that the grain of the stem is not continuous.

85 Wardrobe.

Wardrobes

The eighteenth-century wardrobe had blind panelled doors and three long drawers. Behind the doors will be tray shelves like the Hepplewhite design on p. 34 and there will be graze marks on the inside of the doors where these have rubbed.

This wardrobe was made about 1780; it would fetch today – because of its size – at the most £40. But replace the blind panels of the door with 13 panes of glass each, and replace the drawers with two doors (made from the panels) and you will have a 'china-cabinet' that will fetch £800–900. Or you could add a wing to either side and turn it into a break-front-bookcase.

86 Wine-coolers.

Wine-coolers

The genuine wine-cooler, like these, had the stand made of laminated wood for extra strength. If you can find one you will be fortunate indeed.

Remember, too, that the timber must be the same in the lid and body (and under the brass bands).

The original eighteenth-century wine-cooler was plain. In Victorian times people often had them inlaid with a cockleshell or some other ornament. This work was often done by the local undertaker, the nearest there was to a cabinet-maker.

Wine-coolers are popular and widely manufactured.

PART SIX

The Museum of Naughty Pieces

Every week some reproduction of a work of art is passed off as the genuine article. In some cases, the dealer is unaware of the innate fraud—he himself never suspected deception, and wouldn't be able to detect deception if it were cleverly enough executed.

In the following pages, a number of such "naughty" pieces of furniture are shown. Each of these frauds or partial frauds or reproductions or counterfeits — depending upon the strength of your feelings or upon the degree of misrepresentation—has fooled one or more buyers who have plunked down a sizeable amount of money in the belief that they were buying the authentic, original article.

It isn't at all easy to detect the lack of authenticity of these pieces of furniture. In many cases, although they are not original 18th-century pieces, they have undoubted charm. There is no gainsaying the esthetic appeal of a number of these counterfeits. But we are not concerned with that aspect here. One may choose to buy a reproduction, with full awareness that it is not an antique but that is quite different from buying a reproduction in the belief that one is acquiring a genuine antique. We simply would like you to view this museum of naughty pieces, so that you may be privy to the secret that reproductions are, in many cases, done so cleverly that they can fool any but the most knowledgeable connoisseur.

87 This chair was made from a settee.

88 Why is this piece "naughty?" Look at the front, and you will see how the grain of the timbers continues through the inlaid lines, proving that the inlay has been added after the piece was made. Look, too, at the plinth which is disproportionately narrow for the size of the piece, and obviously not original. The desk has ivory escutcheons, and escutcheons were never used on desks before Victorian times.

89 Arms coming out of the back of a genuine 18th-century chair. These arms must have been added.

90 Here is another marriage. This is given away by the fact that the grain on the sides of the top and the grain on the sides of the bottom run different ways, instead of the same way. This fact is evidence that the two pieces were not made for each other. Note the bandages, or spats, above the castors. The purpose of these is to add an extra inch or so to make the piece reach the correct height for writing. The open grain of the top piece shows that this satin wood dates from Victorian times.

91 This is a Sheraton design executed in yellow satinwood with open grain, a wood not used until Victorian times. The painting is modern. The give-away is the open grain of the timber.

92 This used to be a washstand, but has been converted into a dressing table. The square glass is obviously not 18th-century, and who would put those filials on the mirror frame? This conversion may be a perfectly nice piece of furniture, but it is not a genuine 18th-century piece.

93   The arms of the single chair have been added. The piece on the right
of the chair used to be the top of a tallboy when it had four long drawers.
The give-away: the columns at the side. Moreover, the drawers are wrong
for a chest of drawers.

94 In this piece, one escutcheon is Victorian (square bottom), and the escutcheon
rounded at the bottom is of another period. The Victorian escutcheon could, of
course, be a replacement; but it is highly doubtful that the inlay would have been
designed to be cut by the top and bottom of the top drawer, as it is here. There is
no doubt in my mind that this inlay is an addition, even if the rest of the piece is
genuine.

95 Although sold several times as a Sheraton piece, this sideboard is pure Victorian. The spade feet are perhaps the ugliest thing about this immense sideboard. The piece certainly has none of the grace and elegance of the 18th century.

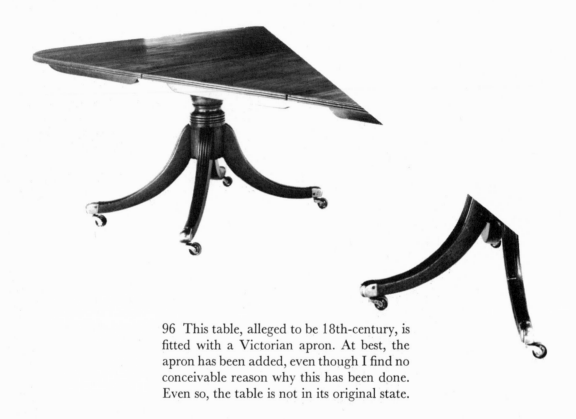

96 This table, alleged to be 18th-century, is fitted with a Victorian apron. At best, the apron has been added, even though I find no conceivable reason why this has been done. Even so, the table is not in its original state.

97 Another top part of a tallboy. The give-away is again the feet. These are monstrosities, the sight of which would make any 18th-century cabinet maker pall. The
lifting handles, a later addition, should be in the middle—not two-thirds of the way
up the side. The handles on the drawers are much later in design than the piece they
are on. The whole has been reveneered.

98. This supposed bureaux-bookcase is a marriage. The doors of the top part have two hinges, instead of the three they would have had if genuine. The escutcheons of the top and bottom are

different, showing that they were not made for each other originally. In actual face, the cornice, originally on a wardrobe, has been made more shallow.

99 Square top corners show that this mirror,
if 18th-century, is not in its original state.

100 Hunting tables are Victorian and can never be correctly labelled 18th-century. The genuine hunting table has four round legs that screw in and out—never tripods as here. Tripods would not stand on uneven ground nor fit into a waggon.

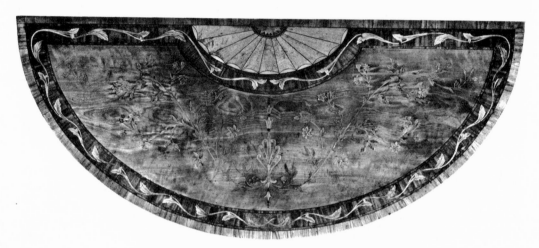

101   This is a top of a genuine 18th-century drawing-room commode. The open grain shows that the piece has been stripped and re-waxed. The cross-banding is genuine, but the painted design has been added after stripping. In the 18th century, no one would have dreamed of painting over cross-banding. A painted design in the vacant space is just conceivable.

102   This sideboard has butterfly hinges attached to the front, instead of pin-hinges which were used for this type of piece in the 18th century. The feet are modern. As can be seen, these feet are much wider than the 18th-century styles. There is no pretence that the leg and the foot are of one piece, as they should be. This is a Victorian piece that started life with ugly feet that proclaimed its origin, so the feet were changed, and the piece now passes for Regency.

103   As far as the bottom of the top drawer, this sideboard is all right. An early Victorian piece—which it is—it used to have six circular ugly legs, but these have been replaced with eight bracket feet. When the two bottom drawers were added, the sides were reveneered. You can see that there is different timber in the top. Compare this wood to that of the sides and the bottom.

Glossary of Timbers

Amboyna
From East and West India, used as veneer and inlay, the burls are light and reddish brown, highly mottled and curled. Known and used in furniture since Roman times.

Applewood
The wood of the apple tree is very hard, is a brown-pink colour and polishes well. Used for small pieces of furniture and is ideal for turning.

Ash
A family of trees which include olive, lilac, privet and jasmine.

The olive ash burls of England are exquisitely figured and capable of beautiful veneer matching. The wood is a very light creamy colour, heavy and dense with a grain that resembles oak. It was often used for legs and turnings of early Windsor chairs.

Beech
From Europe and America, dense texture, light colour, used in poor quality work, mainly country pieces, polishes well to light brown colour.

Birch
Wood family of many varieties found in temperate zones, the white and sap birches are soft, the red, black and yellow are hard. It was used everywhere for furniture and was very cheap.

The harder varieties have great strength and polish well, often used to imitate mahogany.

Boxwood
Is the only English timber that will sink in water, has a fine grain, and is yellow in colour, used mainly for inlays.

Brazil Wood
Comes from East India. Light colour and used mainly for inlays.

Calamander
From Ceylon. Used in England in the late eighteenth century, is very heavy and has a black streak.

Camphor
From the East Indies and was mainly used for small things like boxes.

Cedar
From North America and the West Indies, is red and smells nice, was used for boxes and drawer linings and the moths hate it.

Cherry
Is very hard and has a fine grain, is a light red brown in colour, and will not warp, always polishes nicely. In England in 1664 it was used a great deal for inlay work.

Chestnut
Soft greyish brown in colour with coarse open grain which resembles oak, was used mainly for veneers.

Cinnamon
Is the same as Camphor.

Coromandel
Bombay Ebony from the Coromandel coast, blackish rosewood in texture, with light stripes.

Cypress
Dark red wood of very hard texture, valued for its durability. Cypress chests were made as early as the fourteenth century.

Deal
English name for Pine particularly the Scotch Pine, the name is a Dutch term for part, signifying the division of boards when used for cores in veneering.

Ebony
Tropical wood of general black colour, heavy and dense in texture.

Elm
The wood of this family is generally of very light brown colour and a porous, oak-like texture, it was used for furniture by the Romans and there are surviving Gothic examples.

English chairs of elm, particularly with elm seats, were made in large numbers in the eighteenth century.

Harewood
English. Is dyed or stained Sycamore and is a greenish-grey in colour. It was first used in England in the eighteenth century and chiefly used for inlays and decorative veneering. After a few years the dyes faded and left just a green colour.

Holly
Hard, greyish-white wood and is one of the whitest of all woods, with a small flecked grain, used mainly for inlays, many pieces of oak were inlaid with Holly.

Kingwood
From South America. Dark reddish brown wood similar to Rosewood, was used for inlays on flat surfaces, mainly late Georgian.

Laburnum
Is a hard wood, yellowish in colour with brown streaks, it takes a high polish, in ancient Rome it was called Corsican Ebony. It was used as veneer.

Lignum
West Indian wood, the heaviest known, it was used for veneering in the late Stuart period.

Lime
Light coloured, close-grained wood which cuts equally well across as with the grain, rendering it excellent for carving, and Grinling Gibbons, the carver, loved to use it.

Mahogany
Reddish brown wood of medium hardness, great strength and among the most beautiful for texture, is easy to polish and has a variety of grain and figure. Today Mahogany includes several botanical species, chiefly the Swietenia of the West Indies, South and Central America, and the Khaya of Africa.

The American mahoganies were the first known.

Spanish explorers were quick to appreciate its splendid properties, and its early importation and use in cabinet work is attested by the sixteenth-century date of some fine Spanish Renaissance remains.

Queen Elizabeth is said to have been very interested in the mahogany that Sir Walter Raleigh brought in, but it was not in favour in England until the eighteenth century.

In 1733 the heavy tariff against mahogany was modified, and it quickly supplanted other woods in fine work and held its ascendancy for many years. The Cuban and San Domingan varieties were preferred as these had a hard firm texture which carved well. It started a light colour and changed slowly to a deep, rich lustrous tone, and with the different figures such as rope, fiddleback, etc. stimulated the designer's imagination.

Later the Mexican mahoganies came on the market with their own special characteristics.

In the late nineteenth century the African varieties were accepted as true mahogany, but are lighter in weight and do not have nice figuring.

From the eighteenth century, England, France, America, Spain and Italy used mahogany continually. In England we polished mahogany with bees' wax which was red tinted and gave the wood a nice light red-brown colour, the French Empire wood was a rich dark red and highly polished.

Maple

From the Acer family mainly from America. It has fine structural properties and is very decorative. There are hard and soft varieties with unusual figures and textures, some are curly bird's eye and quilted figures, it was used in the solid lumbers or as veneers. It has a high ratio of strength and very seldom splits, honey in colour.

Oak

This wood is hard and heavy, the colour varying from white to brown according to the soil, the position of the tree in the forest and the period of seasoning in water.

At the close of the seventeenth century, oak was only used for drawer linings and carcase work of the best quality veneered pieces, but country pieces were still made of oak.

The extensive forests of Britain were thickly stocked with oak and for a long time the mature timber was felled in great quantities and planting did not keep pace with consumption, and because of the alarming reduction of our forests, an Act of War was passed under Henry VIII enforcing the preservation of oak woods.

By the middle of Elizabeth's reign, the planting of oaks had become common but these would not be mature until the late seventeenth or early eighteenth century.

In late Tudor and Jacobean work we find that a lot of the oak used was imported from Germany. This was softer and whiter than the English oak.

Until the two-handed saws were used in the sixteenth century, the conversion of the oak trunk into smaller sizes was done by splitting the wood, but a saw must have been used in converting trees of a great age and also those which had had the sap dried out after felling, as nearly always the oak was split while the timber was green and then left to season in a stream or river. Sometimes this took as long as two years.

The oak was always slow-growing and took between 150 and 200 years to mature.

Olive Wood

Is a hard, close-grained wood, greenish-yellow in colour with dark markings, it takes a hard polish and is used for veneers and inlays on pieces of Stuart furniture and English Regency furniture.

Pyster Pieces
Veneers cut as cross sections of roots and branches of some trees like walnut and laburnum saplings. The rings resemble oyster shells. Used on many William and Mary pieces.

Padouk or Andaman
Is from Burma and looks like rosewood, came here early in the eighteenth century and was used very often for fretwork.

Partridge Wood
From Brazil and used in parquetry and inlaid work, it is closely grained and heavy and is brownish-red in colour.

Pine
A lot was grown in Scotland. It is a soft wood and was liked by the carvers and gilders. It was used mostly for carcase work, it is a whitish-yellow colour.

Plane Wood
Is a maple-leafed London Plane, is white in colour and very hard, was used for flys on Pembroke tables.

Plumb Wood
Yellowish wood with a deep brown heart, is hard and heavy. Little used after 1700.

Poplar
Pale yellowish colour, very soft and light in weight, was used mostly for inlays.

Purple Wood
From Brazil, looks like Rosewood, has black stripes and was used for crossbanding.

Rosewood
From India and Brazil. It got its name because when freshly cut it smells like roses. It is heavy and is red brown in colour. Was used as veneers in the eighteenth century and for solid furniture in the nineteenth century.

Satinwood
From East and West Indies. Is yellow in colour and the West Indian is the best because it is finely figured.

Sycamore
Also known as Maple and when dyed, known as Harewood. Used for veneers. Light in colour.

Teak
From the East, very heavy, light brown in colour with a straight grain, was used a lot in the East.

Thuya
Is from Africa, is warm brown in colour with wavy lines, used mainly for veneers.

Tulip
From Brazil. Is light brown and has wide stripes of red and was used for veneers on a lot of Regency pieces.

Walnut
It is very strong and has many colours, figures, burls and waves and was fashionable in England until 1730.

Yew
Red brown wood, takes a hard polish, used a lot on country-made pieces.

Zebrawood
From British Guiana, called because of its brown stripes on a yellow base. Used mainly for crossbanding.